C000242085

LEARNING FOR LIFE & WORK

LOCAL AND GLOBAL CITIZENSHIP

FOR CCEA GCSE

COLOURPOINT
EDUCATIONAL

Paula McCullough

© Paula McCullough and Colourpoint Books 2011

ISBN: 978 1 906578 71 8

First Edition
Second Impression, 2015

Layout and design: April Sky Design, Newtownards
Printed by: GPS Colour Graphics Ltd, Belfast

All rights reserved. No part of this publication
may be reproduced, stored in a retrieval
system or transmitted in any form or by any
means, electronic, mechanical, photocopying,
scanning, recording or otherwise, without
the prior written permission of the copyright
owners and publisher of this book.

Copyright has been acknowledged to the
best of our ability. If there are any inadvertent
errors or omissions, we shall be happy to
correct them in any future editions.

Page 112 constitutes an extension of this
copyright page.

The Author

Paula McCullough has over 23
years experience of teaching
in Northern Ireland and
examining at GCSE, AS and A2
Level. She is currently head
of the Religious Education
Department at Methodist
College Belfast and also
teaches LLW to GCSE level.

Acknowledgements

For Citizenship, I have had the privilege of working with
two editors. Michael Spence started the book with me
and Rachel Irwin saw it through to completion. Many
thanks, both of you, for your guidance, support and
meticulous work.

I would also like to thank Colourpoint for giving me the
opportunity to write this series for LLW and to Jill Armer
at CCEA for her help and advice.

Whilst writing this book I asked some people to
contribute to the text by sharing their own thoughts and
experiences. Many thanks to those of you who assisted
in this way; I am especially grateful to my Form 4 pupils
who agreed to help.

Finally, the whole writing process was made easier by the
support of my family, husband Frazer and sons Peter and
Michael. Peter took the author photograph and Michael
was my technical assistant when laptop difficulties arose.

COLOURPOINT
EDUCATIONAL

Colourpoint Educational
An imprint of Colourpoint Creative Ltd
Colourpoint House
Jubilee Business Park
21 Jubilee Road
Newtownards
County Down
Northern Ireland
BT23 4YH

Tel: 028 9182 6339
Fax: 028 9182 1900
E-mail: sales@colourpoint.co.uk
Web site: www.colourpoint.co.uk

Whilst the publisher has taken all reasonable care in the
preparation of this book CCEA makes no representation,
express or implied, with regard to the accuracy of the
information contained in this book. CCEA does not
accept any legal responsibility for any errors or omissions
from the book or the consequences thereof.

CONTENTS

		Page

What is Citizenship?

Citizenship is about the relationship between an individual and the community in which he or she lives.

A citizen is a member of a social, political or national community. Citizenship involves each person taking an active role in this community. This can mean working towards improving society, perhaps through voluntary work, or taking a responsibility seriously, such as voting in an election.

A citizen has certain rights and obligations. Citizenship is about making sure that everyone understands what these are and can take a full role in society. It also involves being aware of the rights and freedoms of others.

Citizenship is not just concerned with the relationships we have with others locally, but also nationally and globally.

Chapter one

DIVERSITY AND INCLUSION IN NORTHERN IRELAND AND THE WIDER WORLD

CHAPTER SUMMARY

In this chapter you will be studying:

- Cultural diversity and cultural identity in Northern Ireland.
- The positive contribution made by different ethnic groups.
- Challenges faced by immigrants, migrant workers and refugees.
- Methods of resolving conflict.
- Ways to promote a more inclusive society.

CULTURAL DIVERSITY IN N. IRELAND

WHAT IS CULTURAL DIVERSITY?

Look around at your classmates and the people in your local community and you can probably see cultural diversity for yourself! The population of Northern Ireland is changing. People are coming to live here from all over the world and this has the potential to make our society more vibrant and interesting. Thai restaurants, Salsa dance classes, Indian festivals and Polish food shops are just some of the many ways in which people can enjoy new experiences. Cultural diversity is to be welcomed. It is a sign of a tolerant and understanding community that people from different cultural, religious and racial backgrounds can live alongside each other without misunderstanding or prejudice.

Cultural diversity can be seen in a global as well as local context. People around the world are more connected to each other than ever before, largely due to advances in technology. International travel is more frequent and available to more people, so there are greater opportunities to meet others from different cultures.

─TO THINK ABOUT...─

· Consider the past week. Have there been any ways in which your life might have been influenced by different cultures? Think about the food you have eaten, activities you have taken part in and films and television programmes you have watched.

· Are we sometimes influenced by other cultures without even realising it?

In my experience

"*Diversity is a good thing! Living in a mixed society allows people to be more open and tolerant towards other cultures. My own family is very diverse, from the occasional speaking of Gaelic to celebrating Chinese New Year. My father is from Hong Kong, while my mother is Northern Irish and my relatives include people who are Buddhist, Christian and Muslim. I see myself as both Irish and Chinese,*

as well as being Catholic. In my opinion, people in Northern Ireland are fairly tolerant of minority groups who have been here for many years, such as the Chinese community, although I have experienced some racist name-calling. I think people who have arrived in Northern Ireland more recently are probably more likely to be the target of racism."

— **Brandon, aged 15**

WHAT IS AN ETHNIC GROUP?

An **ethnic group** is a group of people whose members identify with each other because they share something in common, such as their religion or country of origin. **Cultural identity** is the sense of belonging to this group. Cultural identity is not exclusive and people may identify with more than one ethnic group. **Ethnicity** can be defined by race, language, food, music and traditions. An **ethnic minority** is any ethnic group which are relatively small in number in the area where they are living. A society where the people come from many different ethnic groups is described as having '**cultural diversity**'.

Some people might assume that being a member of an ethnic minority group simply means that a person is not 'white'. However, there are a number of factors that can determine which ethnic group a person identifies with, including racial, religious, cultural, political, national and linguistic distinctions.

5

Invite a guest speaker from an ethnic minority group to come and speak to your class. Everyone could prepare questions in advance, which could be emailed to the speaker beforehand.

The following list gives just some examples of different ethnic minorities living in Northern Ireland:

African Caribbean

This is a relatively small ethnic group, with around 1,500 people of African-Caribbean origin who have either settled here or are students. There is no single African-Caribbean community – members of this ethnic group come from many different parts of the African continent and Caribbean Islands, each with their own distinct culture. In 1995, the Northern Ireland African Cultural Centre was set up to provide services and support for the African-Caribbean community. Most members of this ethnic group are from a Christian background.

Bahá'í

The Bahá'í faith is one of the world's youngest religions. It started in Persia in the middle of the nineteenth century and now has over 5 million followers throughout the world. In Northern Ireland there is a fairly small but active Bahá'í community of just over 300 people. Members of the Bahá'í community represent a wide range of backgrounds, ages and cultures. Some Bahá'ís have come from other countries, such as Iran, while others are local people who have converted to the faith. The Bahá'í community comes together to worship every nineteen days, which is the length of a Bahá'í month. The governing body of the Bahá'ís is called a Spiritual Assembly. The Belfast Spiritual Assembly celebrated its 50th anniversary in 2000 at Belfast Castle.

Chinese

Chinese people started to arrive in Northern Ireland in the 1960s, so they are one of the first racial minority groups to settle here. The Chinese community is now one of the largest ethnic groups, with the majority of the Chinese population living in Belfast. It is estimated that there are around 8,000 Chinese people living in Northern Ireland and of this figure 60% were born here.

When Chinese people first settled in Northern Ireland, many opened restaurants and food outlets as a way of earning a living. However, many second and third generation Chinese people are moving away from catering and are following a variety of different careers, including law, medicine and politics. They have better opportunities in education than their parents and grandparents and are fully integrated into the local community. However, language barriers continue to be a problem for many first generation immigrants. As a result, some Chinese residents do not access vital services in health, social care or education.

The Chinese Welfare Association is a voluntary organisation offering help and advice in English, Cantonese and Mandarin. The CWA was established in 1986 as 'The voice and ears of the community'. They aim to provide support for Chinese people who may have problems accessing health or public services. Raising cultural awareness is also an important aim for the CWA as a way of tackling racism. In April 2009, the association secured the first multi-purpose built Chinese community centre in UK, the Chinese Resource Centre. The CWA works across the province and has a branch in Derry which is supported by a local Chinese group, Sai Pak (North West) Chinese Community Association.

Eileen Chan-Hu, Chief Executive, Chinese Welfare Association

"Today the Chinese Community in Northern Ireland is into its third and fourth generation for some. Other, newer, Chinese communities are still in their first generation as they embark upon a journey to make Northern Ireland their home. We work with many Chinese communities of differing origins such as, China, Hong Kong, Taiwan, Singapore and Malaysia and with smaller minority ethnic Chinese regions who have come from as far as Mongolia and Nepal

to Northern Ireland. Chinese Welfare Association supports the Chinese community by becoming a bridge between communities to be part of today's diverse communities in Northern Ireland and in doing so share our culture to enrich and enhance and to be an integral part of Northern Ireland society. In accordance with the Chinese saying, 'What you take from the community, you shall plough back into the community'."

Hindu

Hindus form a small but significant religious group in Northern Ireland. According to official figures from the last census the Hindu population is around 1,000 people. However, the Hindu community themselves think this figure is now currently over 2,000, as their population has increased significantly over the last ten years. Most Hindu families in Northern Ireland originally came here from India and they form part of the larger Indian community.

The first Indians settled in Northern Ireland in the 1930s and many started to earn a living by selling clothes door-to-door. Due to hard work and enterprise, this quickly progressed to ownership of clothes shops. Today, members of the Indian community own factories, shops and restaurants or have followed a different career path, such as medicine, for example.

The Indian Community Centre was opened in 1981. It is located at Carlisle Circus in Belfast in a building that used to be a Methodist Church. The centre is one of the main Hindu places of worship in Belfast, and it also has a number of halls and meeting rooms for community activities. It aims to provide a space for social and religious activities, maintaining the culture and traditions of India. An important aspect of the centre's work is building good relationships with the wider Northern Irish community, through cultural activities and celebrations that are open to everyone.

In my experience

"My nationality is Indian and I have lived in Northern Ireland since I was 5 years old. I think people here are quite tolerant of other cultures and I have never experienced any racism or prejudiced attitudes. Living in a society with people from a variety of backgrounds can help you learn a lot about different cultures and I also believe it helps you become more open-minded. My family is Hindu and we celebrate Christmas, Easter and Halloween just like everyone else here."

Vahsir, aged 15

Jewish

Historical records show that Jewish people have lived in Ireland since the twelfth century and have been in the north of Ireland since at least the seventeenth century. They are therefore the religious minority group who have been here for the longest time. There are an estimated 500 Jewish people living in Northern Ireland today, with around 30 families attending regular worship at the synagogue in North Belfast.

DID YOU KNOW?

• Otto Jaffe was a successful Jewish businessman whose family came to Belfast from Hamburg in 1850. He served for several years as a city councillor and was Lord Mayor of Belfast in 1899 and 1904. He was knighted in 1900.

• Another famous person from the Jewish community was Gustav Wolff. Together with Edward Harland, in 1861, they formed one of the largest ship building companies in the world. The *Titanic* was one of the most famous ships built here.

• During the Second World War, a special project was set up on a farm in Millisle, County Down. Jewish children were rescued from Nazi persecution and brought here to live in safety. The farm saved hundreds of children and one survivor still lives nearby.

Latin American

The term 'Latin American' refers to Spanish and Portuguese speaking countries in South and Central America. There are estimated to be around 200–250 Latin American people living in Northern Ireland. They are mainly young adults, some married with families, who have come here to look for work. Most Latin American people have lived here for only a few years.

Muslim

Most Muslim families in Northern Ireland have come here since the 1920s, although there was a record of a small Muslim population before this. Muslims follow the religion of Islam, so this is a religious group. Many people tend to think all Muslims are from the Middle East, but this is inaccurate as Islam is a worldwide religion. People from any ethnic background can convert to Islam. The Belfast Islamic Centre has estimated that there are between four and five thousand Muslims living in Northern Ireland today. The Muslims in Northern Ireland come from over 40 countries of origin, from Western Europe all the way through to the Far East.

The **Belfast Islamic Centre** was established in 1978 by a group of local Muslims. As well as being a place of worship, it is also a community centre providing services and offering advice. **The Northern Ireland Muslim Family Association** also gives support to local Muslims. Other groups in Ballymena, Coleraine and Lurgan help local Muslims to practice their faith and integrate into the community.

In my experience ~~~~~~~~~

"I have lived here all my life and so I see myself as Northern Irish. I am also a Muslim. My family is originally from India and at home we generally speak our own language, which is Malayalam. We celebrate Muslim festivals, such as Eid and we also observe Ramadan. In my family, we have celebrations at Christmas as well. I think people from different cultures can offer each other new ideas and we can learn about different ways of doing things."

Navid, aged 15

Polish

Compared to some other ethnic minority groups in Northern Ireland, most Polish people here have arrived quite recently. However, they are currently the largest ethnic minority with an estimated population of 30,000 people. Poland joined the European Union in 2004 and since then Polish people have come here to look for work. **The Polish Association NI** was established in 2006. The association supports people who may be experiencing problems, such as language difficulties or discrimination. It also gives information on a variety of topics, for example, health, education and employment. Polish Cultural Week is now held annually in Belfast, as a way of helping local people to experience Polish culture through exhibitions, concerts and films.

Polish Folk Dance
© Brendan Lally

Portuguese

The Portuguese are an ethnic minority group mainly made up of migrant workers, recruited to come and work in Northern Ireland by local factories. After their short-term contract expires they then leave and are replaced by other workers. Most Portuguese people are based in the Portadown area and work in meat processing factories. It is difficult to have accurate statistics for a migrant workforce, but it is thought there are up to 1,500 Portuguese people in Northern Ireland and that most of them are young, single men.

Sikh

The Sikhs are a religious group but they also have racial identity as most of them have family origins in the Punjab, an area in north-west India. Some of the first Sikh immigrants to Northern Ireland arrived in the 1920s, after serving in the British Army. They mostly settled in the city of Derry and the Sikh community today numbers around 200 people. Sikhs are employed in many areas of work, such as medicine, IT and the hotel and catering industry. The Northern Ireland Sikh Association was formed in 1990 and the Sikh Cultural and Community Centre was established in the Waterside district of Derry shortly afterwards.

RESEARCH ACTIVITY

Work in groups of about 4

- Carry out a survey of your school or community and find out how many different ethnic groups are represented.
- Choose one of these groups and research the different ways cultural identity is shown, for example, festivals, celebrations, music, languages spoken, etc.
- Produce a PowerPoint presentation to show to the rest of your class.

Traveller

The Traveller community in Ireland has a distinct ethnic identity which is recognised in law in Northern Ireland and their ethnic history can be traced back for centuries. Traditionally, members of this group were an important part of the rural community in Ireland through horse dealing, blacksmithing, tinsmithing and by providing seasonal labour on farms. There was also a long tradition of the Travellers bringing music and storytelling to the settled communities throughout Ireland before the days of films and television. However, as society became more industrialised in the 1950s, the traditional skills that travellers had to offer were no longer needed.

A 'State of the Art' Traveller site at Acorn Grove, Craigavon

Today, many Travellers try to make a living by dealing in scrap metal, caravan trading or tarmacing. However, a very high percentage of adult Travellers have no employment. There are thought to be around 3,000 Travellers in Northern Ireland, mostly living in the Belfast, Newry, Derry, Craigavon and Dungannon areas.

Belfast City Council is aware of the need to improve quality of life for the Traveller community and have an established Traveller Unit within the Development Department. The Council's *Traveller Liaison Officer, Frank O'Hagan*, is based in the **Traveller Outreach Office** in Belfast and works with the Traveller community on a day to day basis. He describes some of the issues facing Travellers:

"The most important concerns facing the Traveller community are accommodation, health, education, employment and discrimination … the same issues Travellers were facing a decade ago. The key question is WHY? The answer, however, is not an easy one! Some essential services have been promised but not delivered; sometimes Travellers do not take up on opportunities offered to them. Travellers can have low self-esteem and low expectations as they have often been let down in the past. There are now policies in place to ensure Travellers are treated fairly. However, the actual living standards of the Travellers are still lagging far behind that of the settled community. WHY? Attitudes need to change so that members of the Traveller community are treated in the same way as every other citizen of Belfast. The Council's Outreach Office provides an opportunity for service providers and members of the public to meet with the Traveller community in a neutral space. This is a first step in building positive relationships, and it works. Travellers simply want their way of life recognised and understood, including their right to Traveller sites rather than social housing. The Traveller community has a legal right to the services that are available to the settled community, so let us all work together to achieve this goal."

TO THINK ABOUT...

- Why do people from the Traveller community often experience negative attitudes towards their way of life?

- What do you think could be done to change this?

DISCUSSION

Read the following quotes.

"If a minority group expects the same rights as everyone else, then they should try to take an active part in the community in which they live."

"We must respect people who have a different way of life to the rest of us. They are still entitled to the same rights as everyone else."

Discuss both views.

Vietnamese

There are thought to be around 300 people of Vietnamese origin living in Northern Ireland. They arrived here in the 1970s as refugees, fearing persecution in their own country from a communist regime. To escape from Vietnam, they had to undertake a horrific boat journey to Hong Kong, from where they were then resettled in the UK. Most of the families who arrived in Northern Ireland settled in Craigavon. In the early days, language barriers made it difficult for people to find work and they were often the target of racist attacks.

In my experience

"We have been here for twenty years but I am still a refugee. I don't mind us being called 'boat people' because that was a very important part of our lives. I don't mind being called 'refugee' because that is what I am … I think I will be a refugee for the rest of my life and I think my son will be a refugee for the rest of his life because he was four when we left Vietnam but my granddaughter was born here and she is not a refugee … I do have citizenship now and my son has citizenship but we will still be refugees. At least, nobody ever came to tell me that I am not a refugee anymore!"

Source: 'Forced to Flee', publication prepared by the Refugee Action Group (RAG), http://www.workingwithdiversity.org/div/racialgroup/asylumseekersandrefugees.php

Woman refugee originally from Vietnam

People who are members of different ethnic minority groups have various reasons for living here – perhaps fleeing persecution, seeking a better standard of living or simply because they were born here.

Some people are relatively new arrivals, whereas others have lived here for generations. The different ethnic groups represent many different races, nationalities cultures and religions.

RESEARCH ACTIVITY

There are other racial and religious minority groups in Northern Ireland apart from the ones given here.

Use the Internet to find out about the following groups in Northern Ireland:

- Turkish
- Filipino
- Buddhist

What can you discover about the history and cultural identity of each group?

Info Box

SOME USEFUL WEBSITES:

African and Caribbean Association of Foyle: www.acafni.org

Bahá'í Community of the United Kingdom: www.bahai.org.uk

Chinese Welfare Association: www.cwa-ni.org

Indian Community Centre: www.iccbelfast.com

Jewish Belfast.com: www.jewishbelfast.com

Latinoamerica Unida: www.latinoamericaunida.org.uk

Belfast Islamic Centre: www.belfastislamiccentre.org.uk

Polish Association Northern Ireland: www.polskibelfast.pl

Refugee Action Group: www.refugeeactiongroup.com

Irish Travellers Movement in Britain: www.irishtraveller.org.uk

---

ACTIVITY

Read the definition of an ethnic group on page 5. Look at each of the ethnic groups discussed in this section. What is it that gives each of them their own distinct identity? Is it race, religion or something else?

SHOWING CULTURAL IDENTITY

THE 'TWO COMMUNITIES' IN NORTHERN IRELAND

Everyone is part of an ethnic group. Apart from the minority groups that we have looked at, Northern Ireland has been traditionally seen as divided into two distinct groups defined by religion and politics. Members of one group tend to consider themselves Protestant and British, either 'Unionist' or 'Loyalist'. Members of the other group tend to consider themselves Catholic and Irish, either 'Nationalist' or 'Republican'.

The cultural identities of these two main groups are often shown through politics, language, music, traditions and sport – even which football team is supported! However, in Northern Ireland, showing cultural identity has not always been seen as something positive. Particularly during the 'troubles', displays of cultural identity by either Catholic or Protestant groups often caused conflict in the community. Sometimes they were used as a way to threaten and intimidate others.

Wordbox

THE TROUBLES
The troubles in Northern Ireland refers to the three decades of violence that took place towards the end of the last century. This was largely between the Roman Catholic nationalist community and the Protestant unionist community.

Here are some examples:

- **FLAGS** – Many communities are not 'mixed' but are either predominantly Catholic or Protestant. Residents may use the Irish Tricolour or Union Jack as a way of showing this, particularly at certain times of the year.

- **PAINTING AND MURALS** – Kerb stones are sometimes painted to correspond with the colours of a particular flag, again as a way of showing who is the predominant group in a neighbourhood. Murals are sometimes painted on walls or at the end of a terrace, and often show symbols, local heroes or names of paramilitary organisations.

- **MARCHING AND BANDS** – Parades and marches organised by Loyal Orders have played a part in Northern Irish society since the 18th century. For some they are regarded as an important tradition, having a social, political and religious role. Others see the parades as intimidating, and associated with anti-social behaviour. They suggest that marches should be restricted.

- **GRAFFITI** – Political slogans, sometimes in Irish, or names of paramilitary organisations, are another way in which people show the identity of a particular community. Some people think this is intimidating and a way to cause conflict.

DISCUSSION
Which of the examples above could be seen as negative? Explain your reasons to the others in your group.

Religious and political beliefs can be complicated and it is never a good idea to make assumptions about a person. Therefore it can often be misleading to think of Northern Ireland being made up of just 'two communities'.

German, Protestant grandparents

Atheist mother & Catholic Father

Hello, Hola, Hallo

Hurling

Football

Catholic Grammar School

CELEBRATING CULTURAL IDENTITY

Many people consider it important to show their cultural identity. If this is done in a positive way, it can create a strong sense of identity and belonging with a particular group. It can also be an effective way of showing others in the community something of your background and traditions. Joining in with a festival or celebration can be fun and interesting, as well as being a good way to break down barriers and increase understanding. Here are some examples of how cultural identity can be celebrated in a positive way:

Festivals and celebrations

Festival of Colours, St George's Market, Belfast 2010 – Henry Doggart©ArtsEkta.

Classical Indian Dancers entertain at launch of Belfast Mela – Ronnie Moore©ArtsEkta

Chinese New Year

- **Féile an Phobail** is a celebration of Ireland's culture, held each year in August in West Belfast. It is one of Ireland's most popular community festivals. It coincides with the Maiden City Festival, held in the city of Derry, celebrating Ulster-Scots heritage.

- **Holi** is the Hindu festival of colours, celebrated each spring. For a few years now, a special event has been held at St George's Market in Belfast, where everyone can join in the fun with the local Hindu community.

- **Belfast Mela** is a unique summer festival, held in Botanic Gardens in Belfast. This Indian celebration has become a large multi-cultural event, and it attracts around 14,000 people from all communities living in Northern Ireland.

- The **Chinese Welfare Association** promotes the largest Chinese New Year celebrations annually, the Dragonboat Festival and the Mid-Autumn Festival. These events are enjoyed by all communities.

Music and dance

Many people in Northern Ireland enjoy traditional Irish music and dance as a way of showing cultural identity. Dance is important for people of many different ethnic backgrounds. The Indian Community centre organises displays of traditional Indian Dance for visiting school children and members of the public.

ArtsEkta is a voluntary organisation that promotes and celebrates cultural diversity through the arts. It is an organisation that promotes all cultures and prides itself in showcasing innovative projects that will cherish the individual artist and encourage diversity.

ArtsEkta's Festival of Colours celebration in Belfast 2010 – Henry Doggart©ArtsEkta

> "We want to play a part in creating a world where there is no racial discrimination and people of different cultures and backgrounds live and learn together in a supportive environment. ArtsEkta is committed to promoting cultures through the arts."

Source: ArtsEkta, http://www.artsekta.org.uk

Food

All ethnic groups have their own traditional foods, perhaps because they are associated with their country of origin. Some foods have a connection with religious worship or celebrations. Can you think of any examples from your own background?

For Hindus, food is an important part of temple worship and sweet treats called **Prasad** (meaning 'edible gift') are given to worshippers at festival times.

You are probably familiar with Chinese food, but did you know that many traditional Chinese foods are symbolic? When eaten at New Year, these foods have the following meaning:

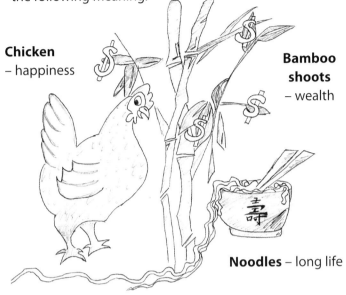

Chicken – happiness

Bamboo shoots – wealth

Noodles – long life

ACTIVITY

Organise an assembly celebrating different cultural groups living in the local community or in Northern Ireland today. You might decide to make this a lunchtime event and have some food available from the different groups represented.

Clothes
Traditional Indian clothes include the **sari** and **shalwar kameez**. Many Indian people living in Northern Ireland choose to wear this traditional dress; others choose to wear 'western' clothes for everyday life and dress traditionally for special occasions. Some would hardly ever wear traditional clothes.

For some Muslim women, wearing a **hijab** is more than just a sign of cultural identity; it is an important religious obligation. Others do not feel that it is important.

In my experience

"Sometimes other pupils in my school ask me "Do your parents make you wear that?" or "Don't you think it really unfair having to dress like that all the time?" I choose to wear the hijab. It is an expression of my identity as a Muslim. I follow what is written in the Qu'ran, and men and women are told to dress modestly."

Amina, aged 14

Language
For many people, language is an important way of showing cultural identity, even if they do not use this language for everyday communication. An example is **Irish**, which is used as a first language by a very small minority of people. However, a growing number of people are using Irish as a second language and choosing to have their children educated through Irish. Irish language schools are known as Bunscoil. Many see the Irish language as an important part of their identity.

The Ulster-Scots Agency is working to promote the use of **Ulster-Scots** as a living language. It runs various summer schools, courses and workshops.

For Muslims, **Arabic** is an essential part of their religious identity, as all worship is carried out in this language. Around 80% of Muslims do not speak Arabic as their first language so they learn it from their parents or at the local mosque from an early age.

"Arabic"

Lifestyle

All families have different ways of doing things and this is especially true when considering families from different ethnic backgrounds. Differences in lifestyle can include the food that is eaten, what languages are spoken at home and family activities.

Sometimes different cultures and traditions can blend together in harmony. Children, in particular can be very adaptable and quickly adjust to a different lifestyle as illustrated below:

"The blend of the Sikhs and Irish culture is more evident in the second generation of Sikhs – who may speak Punjabi at home but perfect their Irish at school; love chips and beans as much as they enjoy Allo-Gobhi and are as busy in their hurling practice as they are in Gurbani lessons. All these children are proud representatives of two cultures at the same time – proof enough that the Sikh and the Irish culture do not contradict each other, but in fact go hand-in-hand and serve to beautifully complement each other."

Source: http://www.irishsikhcouncil.com/IrelandSikhs.htm

ACTIVITIES

Produce a diversity calendar listing the religious and cultural celebrations of various ethnic groups. The Working With Diversity website will help you: www.workingwithdiversity.org/calendar. You will find there are a lot of events happening! Therefore, you might choose to limit the number of groups you decide to include, perhaps to those traditions represented by people in your class or school.

'Just a minute':

Take it in turns to speak for one minute. Your topic is how the group you identify with expresses cultural identity. Only positive methods are allowed!

MAKING A POSITIVE CONTRIBUTION

CHANGES IN POPULATION

Ethnic Groups In Northern Ireland 2001 Census Figures

Ethnic Group	Percentage of persons
White	99.15
Irish Traveller	0.1
Mixed	0.2
Indian	0.09
Pakistani	0.04
Bangladeshi	0.01
Other Asian	0.01
Black Caribbean	0
Black African	0.03
Other Black	0.02
Chinese	0.25
Other Ethnic Group	0.08

*Note: Certain Minority Ethnic representative groups have expressed concern that the census has not yielded accurate data in relation to certain minority ethnic populations because of low participation rates.

Source: Figures from 'Race equality Strategy Consultation Document', Office of the First Minister and deputy First Minister

Wordbox

CENSUS

A census is an official counting of the population, carried out by the government every 10 years.

The population of Northern Ireland is changing as the number of people from ethnic minority groups increases. In the 2001 census, questions were included for the first time about which ethnic group a person identified with. This shows that there is a now recognition that people living in Northern Ireland come from many different ethnic backgrounds.

During the last decade, there has been a growth in the number of European immigrants coming to live in Northern Ireland, as some Central and Eastern European countries have become part of the EU (Economic Union). For example, in 2004 Hungary, Latvia and Lithuania joined the EU giving citizens from these countries the right to seek work in other parts of the EU.

In my experience

"I am Korean and I have lived in Northern Ireland for 10 years. No matter how long I live here, my nationality will always stay the same. On the whole, I think Northern Ireland is a fairly tolerant place to live. However, some people find it hard to see different ways as 'normal' and to accept different people for their community. From time to time, people have called me 'weird' because I do things according to my culture and sometimes people laugh at the way I speak my own language."

Dongmin, aged 16

WHY IS OUR POPULATION CHANGING?

Down through the centuries many immigrants and refugees have chosen to come and live in the UK and the Republic of Ireland. However, until recently, Northern Ireland has never received a significant number of immigrants. This could be because Northern Ireland is one of the most disadvantaged areas of the UK with higher rates of unemployment. It could also be because the violence of the 'troubles' put people off coming to live here. Since the troubles were brought to an end by the peace process, many people from different ethnic groups have chosen to settle here.

OPPORTUNITIES

If cultural diversity is celebrated in a positive way, then this will create many opportunities and benefits for the whole of society.

Here are some examples:

- **Promoting mutual understanding** – Making the effort to learn about another person's customs, lifestyle and religious beliefs can lead to more tolerant attitudes. If you know why a particular custom or practice takes place, then you are more likely to show understanding, rather than prejudice. Understanding is a two-way process, as immigrants also need to learn about the culture of their new country.

- **Understanding other cultures** – Living beside, working with or going to the same school as people from different backgrounds can bring an understanding of different cultures that you cannot get from watching television or reading a book! This understanding is important in today's world where people are far more likely than in the past to have contact with people from different cultures and beliefs.

- **A sense of community spirit** – Shared cultural experiences can be a very effective way of creating community spirit. Some of the examples considered in the previous section – such as the Belfast Mela – are excellent ways of doing this.

- **The community is varied and interesting** – It has often been said that life would be boring if we were all the same. If a community is made up of people from different ethnic backgrounds, then there is much more variety with food, entertainment and shops.

- **The economy receives a boost through new businesses** – Many of the people who come into Northern Ireland want a better life for themselves and their families and they are determined to work hard to achieve this. Many set up businesses to give themselves an income, then as they become more successful, people from the local community are employed, so more jobs are created.

- **Work skills and shortages are eased** – Many skilled and qualified people often choose to leave Northern Ireland for better work opportunities in England, Scotland or overseas. This can leave a shortage of skilled and professional people, such as doctors and other health care workers. People from outside Northern Ireland are coming into the country to fill these posts. Some manual jobs also need to be filled by people from other countries, such as factory or meat processing work.

CHALLENGES

Imagine that your family is moving to a country half way around the world that you know very little about. You may have to adjust to different things.

- **Way of life and culture**: These might seem strange and confusing.

- **Food:** The ingredients for your favourite meal may not be available.

- **Climate:** This can be difficult to get used to, and will also effect what you wear – it may be too hot for your favourite jeans.

- **Language:** At first, you may not being able to read notices or understand what people are saying to you.

Can you think of any others?

These are some of the immediate challenges you could expect when moving to a different country to live – challenges faced by many immigrants when they come to live in Northern Ireland. However, perhaps the most difficult challenge is coping with the attitudes of people towards you, whether misunderstanding, prejudice, hostility or racism. People from ethnic minority groups who were born here and who are fully integrated into society still have this challenge to face.

Here are some examples of challenges to be faced:

- **Language barriers** – Some people might arrive with only a little English, which can make it very difficult to cope with daily life. This can be a particular problem for women who stay at home to care for the family. While the rest of the family can learn English through school and work, she will probably have less contact with people speaking English. Many of the organisations supporting immigrants and refugees believe that language classes for women are a priority.

- **Access to resources and public services** – Some simple and essential things such as registering with a doctor, enrolling children into a local school or finding a place to live can be very daunting for a person who is new to the country and trying to cope with language barriers at the same time.

- **Myths and prejudiced attitudes** – Many people from ethnic minority groups have to face the challenge of other people's ignorance and prejudice towards their culture, lifestyle or religion. This can take the form of name-calling, discrimination, or even violence. The challenge for everyone in society is to try and be as well-informed and tolerant as possible towards people from a different background.

- **Community tension** – If problems arise, perhaps due to misunderstanding, or barriers of language and culture, then it is the responsibility of the whole community to make sure that these are dealt with. The challenge for everyone is to resolve conflict, rather than resorting to violence, which only causes greater mistrust and division.

DISCUSSION

- What are some of the challenges presented by a diverse population?
- What fears and concerns might some people have when immigrants and migrant workers live and work alongside them?
- How could the whole community benefit if immigrants are welcomed and valued?

Dr Mamoun Mobayed is former Chairman of both the Belfast Islamic Centre and the Northern Ireland Muslim Family Association. He describes some of the challenges faced by Muslims living in Northern Ireland:

"It is to be expected that Muslims, like any other minority group, will have challenges to face living in Northern Ireland. Islam is a complete way of life for Muslims, not just a religion. This means that all Muslims have to think carefully about daily life, behaviour and dealings with other people.

Muslims have to observe five prayer times during the day, two of which occur during working hours. Some schools or workplaces do not have a suitable quiet space to offer for prayer.

Muslims are not allowed to drink alcohol. This might cause social embarrassment as many Muslims will not feel very comfortable going to a pub or disco. Muslims are not supposed to have any sexual relations before marriage and people find it strange that Muslim boys and girls do not have girlfriends or boyfriends!

Both men and women have to dress modestly, and women to cover their hair by wearing the 'hijab'. However, some people have a negative attitude towards this, which can put pressure on girls and women.

Boys and girls cannot take part in swimming sessions or other sporting activities where the sexes are mixed or where individual changing rooms are not available!

Despite these challenges, Muslims live happily and peacefully in Northern Ireland. There are a few things which can help Muslims integrate into the local community. Islam is, to some extent, a flexible faith which takes on board positive local practices, providing they are not forbidden or harmful. The time of prayer does not have to be rigid. Islam encourages its followers to relate well to their neighbours and contribute to the welfare of the community.

It helps Muslims a lot when schools, employers and community services have some understanding of Muslims and the Islamic way of life."

RESEARCH ACTIVITY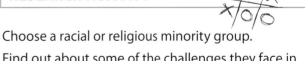

Choose a racial or religious minority group.

Find out about some of the challenges they face in living in Northern Ireland.

What help is available to help overcome difficulties?

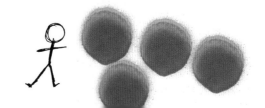

CASE STUDY – NICEM

The Northern Ireland Council for Ethnic Minorities is a voluntary group based in Belfast, although their work covers the whole of Northern Ireland. NICEM helps people from ethnic minority groups cope with some of the challenges they face in their daily lives.

Vision & Mission

"Our vision is of a society where equality and diversity are respected, valued and embraced, a society free from all forms of racism, sectarianism, discrimination and social exclusion; where human rights are guaranteed. NICEM works in partnership, to bring about social change through partnership and alliance building, and to achieve equality of outcome and full participation in society."

NICEM's work includes:

- **Campaigning** – NICEM campaigns for effective laws to promote human rights and equality. It is working to put an end to racial discrimination.

- **Support to migrant workers** – Migrant workers arriving in Northern Ireland can have many problems to face, such as language barriers. NICEM gives advice and support on many different issues.

- **Support to victims of racial harassment** – NICEM says hate crime is one of the most serious issues facing ethnic minority groups, and this includes racial bullying at school. NICEM gives practical advice and support to those who have been the victim of a racial attack or discrimination.

- **Anti-Racism Training** – NICEM's training aims to give an awareness of the value of cultural diversity and promote understanding between people of different backgrounds.

For more information visit the NICEM website: www.nicem.org.uk

CHECK YOUR LEARNING

1. Look at the information about different ethnic minority groups (pages 5–11). Make a list of reasons why people might come to Northern Ireland.

2. Why is the make-up of Northern Ireland's population changing?

3. What is meant by the terms '**cultural diversity**' and '**ethnic group**'?

4. What are some of the advantages of living in a society with people of many different ethnic origins?

5. Some groups have been here for years (they are 'second' or 'third generation' immigrants, depending on whether they or their parents were born here) while others are new arrivals. What different problems could be faced by each group? How do the problems compare?

You could present your answer in the form of a table, such as the one below:

PROBLEM/DIFFICULTY	NEW ARRIVALS	SECOND/THIRD GENERATION
Language barriers		
Discrimination		

6. Write a short paragraph to summarise the work of NICEM.

evaluation

Evaluate the impact of immigration on Northern Ireland society.

DIVISION AND CONFLICT

DIVISION AND CONFLICT

Expressions of cultural identity can sometimes be misunderstood or seen by others in a negative way. This can lead to division in the community between people of different cultural identities. In a divided community the mutual understanding and respect needed between different groups is often lacking. In a situation such as this, conflicts are more likely to arise and can be more difficult to resolve. The result is even greater division and mistrust, resulting in prejudice and stereotyping. Sectarianism and racism quickly develop in situations such as these.

This is shown in the following diagram:

5. PREJUDICE, STEREOTYPING, RACISM AND SECTARIANISM

1. EXPRESSION OF CULTURAL IDENTITY IS SEEN NEGATIVELY

4. CONFLICT, HOSTILITY AND MISTRUST

2. DIVISION IN THE COMMUNITY; LACK OF MUTUAL UNDERSTANDING

3. BREAKDOWN IN COMMUNITY RELATIONSHIPS AND INCREASE IN TENSION

definitions

Prejudice

The word 'prejudice' literally means to 'pre-judge' someone. This means that you have already made your mind up about a person, or group of people before you really know anything about them. Prejudice is therefore a judgement based on

ignorance. Prejudice concerns a person's thoughts rather than their actions.

Where does prejudice come from?

- **It is a natural instinct** – People tend to feel safe with those who are from a similar background and share the same views. Therefore, anyone who is outside this group can appear strange or threatening.

- **It is learnt from an early age** – Many children grow up with racist or sectarian views because they learn them from their parents or the community they grow up in.

- **It is the result of experience** – A person may receive bad treatment from someone of a different racial, religious or ethnic group. This may lead them to think negatively of other people from the same background.

Discrimination

Discrimination occurs when a person puts their prejudiced thoughts into action. Discrimination involves treating a person or group of people less favourably because of culture, race, religion, gender, sexual orientation or disability. There are laws in place in our society to try to ensure that discrimination does not affect a person's right to be treated fairly in education, employment and society.

DISCUSSION

Work in groups of about 4 for this activity.
- How many different types of prejudice or discrimination can you think of?
- Each person in the group should have an opportunity to describe a situation when they felt discriminated against. How did this experience make you feel?

Stereotyping

A stereotype is a crude mental picture that a person might have of someone from another culture. Like prejudice, stereotypes are usually based on ignorance. If you assume that everyone in a particular ethnic group is the same, then you probably do not know many people from that group!

ACTIVITY

Write (or draw) a stereotyped view of yourself. This means you have to imagine that everyone with the same first name as you is exactly the same – likes and dislikes, physical characteristics, character, abilities, and so on. For example, *'All people called Sean are good at football, have blond hair and hate Brussels sprouts.'*

Compare your stereotype with others in your class – especially those who have the same name as you! What does this show about stereotypes?

Scapegoat

A scapegoat is someone who is blamed for the wrongs someone else has committed. The idea comes from the Bible, when the Jewish High Priest would symbolically lay all the sins of the people on a goat and send it out into the wilderness. People often find it easier to blame others for their problems, and it is often members of ethnic minority groups who end up being the scapegoat.

EXAMPLE
The Holocaust shows the consequences of stereotyping and using others as a scapegoat.
After the First World War, many people in Germany suffered from unemployment and a low standard of living. Hitler needed a **scapegoat** so he blamed the Jews, who were a religious minority group. This led to the Holocaust, a systematic attempt

to wipe out the Jewish population through the death camps. Hitler convinced many people that the Jews deserved to be treated in this way as he had **stereotyped** them as being 'sub-human' through a campaign that used anti-Jewish posters and films. As a result, over 6 million Jews died in the Holocaust.

Racism

Racism involves both **prejudice** (an attitude based on ignorance) and **discrimination** (treating a person unfairly because of a prejudiced view). Racism is the belief that one race of people is superior to another. As a person's race might influence their skin colour, language, nationality and culture, racism can involve discrimination because of any of these factors. Racial harassment is also a form of racism. It can involve verbal abuse, graffiti and damage to property.

Sectarianism

There are many ways of grouping people. Sometimes within a larger racial or national group, people are sub-divided into smaller groups. Sectarianism is prejudice or discrimination directed towards someone who is a member of a smaller group within the same race or nationality. Sectarian tensions can be seen between some Catholic and Protestant groups in Northern Ireland, or between Sunni Muslims and Shi'a Muslims.

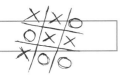
Work in groups of about 4

- Choose either **sectarianism** or **racism**.
- Discuss the **causes** and **effects** for the whole of society and for individual people.
- In your group, produce two spider diagrams on a large sheet of paper, one for **causes** and one for **effects**.
- Share your ideas with the rest of the class.

ACTIVITY
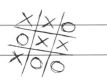

THE SINGH FAMILY

Mr and Mrs Singh have lived in Northern Ireland for nearly sixteen years. Their two children, Ciara and Bobby, were born here. The Singhs have a good relationship with their neighbours and many friends in the local community. A recent attack on their property has made them worried. Someone spray-painted 'Go home' on their garden fence and their car was splattered with broken eggs and rubbish.

- Mr Singh is very angry and wants to call the police. "This is a racial hate crime" he says, "those responsible shouldn't get away with it. Next time it could be a lot worse."

- Mrs Singh, is also upset but she is trying not to show it. She gets on well with her neighbours and does not want to make a fuss. This attack must surely have been made by someone from outside the area.

- 14 year old Ciara has taken her mother's side and is demanding her father does nothing, "Dad, this is just so embarrassing and you are going to make it even worse. Now everyone will be talking about it in school!"

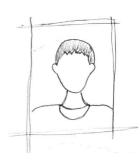

- 11 year old Bobby has suggested that he could get extra pocket money for cleaning the car, then goes out to play football with his friends.

1. What are the different courses of action that the Singh family could take?

2. What are the possible outcomes of each course of action?

3. What do you think would be best for the whole family?

DISCUSSION

In what ways does sectarianism affect the whole of society in Northern Ireland?

23

DISCUSSION
Here are some comments you might have heard before.

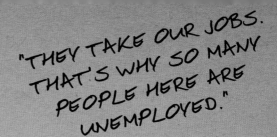

"They take our jobs. That's why so many people here are unemployed."

"Some migrant workers are brought into Northern Ireland because of labour shortages in local factories."

"Many people from ethnic minority groups set up their own businesses when they arrive in the country to support themselves and their families. This often creates new jobs and many now provide employment for local people."

"They only come here to claim benefits."

"Many new arrivals would not qualify for state benefits."

"People who come to Northern Ireland usually do so because they are determined to make a better life for themselves and their families. This means they are prepared to work hard to achieve this."

"They're putting pressure on our public services. Waiting lists in hospitals are going to get longer. I think local people should be treated first!"

"Many doctors, nurses and healthcare workers in Northern Ireland are from ethnic minority groups because we have a shortage of skilled people to fill these posts."

"Without them, waiting lists would be even longer!"

In groups of 4 discuss the comments above.

- Individually, write down the comments that you agree with (if any).
- Taking it in turns, explain to the rest of the group why you agree with these comments.
- Are there any comments that no one agrees with? If so discuss why people may have these views.
- Finally, evaluate the evidence to support each comment.

ACTIVITY

Look at the comments opposite.

Are any of these an example of the following:

   a) stereotyping

   b) discrimination

   c) treating people as scapegoats?

SOURCES OF CONFLICT

There are many sources of conflict existing within societies today – religion, culture, politics, race, ethnic background and social inequalities are some examples of them.

- **Conflict simply means a disagreement or difference.** There can sometimes be conflict when different cultures come together as they may not hold the same values or follow the same traditions. Conflicts can arise if a particular group feel that their rights are being overlooked or denied.

- **Conflict can have a positive outcome.** Perhaps a problem is solved or a misunderstanding is sorted out. How the conflict is handled by all people involved is important.

- **Conflict can lead to violence.** If a conflict is based on fear of the other person's difference, then for some people violence might be a first reaction. Violence has a negative impact on individuals and the whole of the community. Through examining the causes of conflict, it should be possible to work out a positive solution that does not involve violence.

ACTIVITY

Work individually or in pairs.

Use the Internet or newspapers to find examples of recent conflicts at home and overseas. Try to find an example of one local, one national and one global conflict.

For each example identify:

  1. How the conflict started.

  2. Who is involved in the conflict.

  3. The different opinions each group or person represents.

  4. The reasons for the conflict.

  5. Ways in which the conflict could be resolved.

Consider all your examples. Are there any similarities between them?

RESOLVING CONFLICT

CONFLICT RESOLUTION

When differences of opinion, disputes and conflicts arise between groups of people, there are constructive ways of dealing with them. Some people seem to respond to any conflict or disagreement with violence and aggression, but this causes damage on both sides of the disagreement and does not resolve any issues.

The term **conflict resolution** refers to a range of methods for getting rid of sources of conflict. These usually involve **negotiation** and **mediation** – in other words, people talking to each other and working out a solution that is acceptable to everybody involved.

Many conflicts can be resolved successfully through informal discussion or **negotiation** by the people involved. If this does not happen for any reason, then mediation is the next stage. **Mediation** is about helping people to communicate on a difficult issue. A 'mediator', who will not be seen as taking sides, is usually involved to improve understanding between the two groups and help them talk to each other. A mediator needs to be very careful to avoid creating any more tensions. The aim is to think creatively and come to decisions that both parties can agree to.

CASE STUDY – CONFLICT RESOLUTION IN COMBER, CO DOWN

"Comber hit the headlines several years ago for all the wrong reasons when Lithuanians and local people clashed, resulting in a riot on the main street. The Comber Diversity Project was set up by Ards Borough Council and Mediation Northern Ireland to respond to increasing tension in the area. And now the group hopes that the project could help other communities that are struggling to build relationships between local people and migrants moving into the area."

Brent van der Linde from Mediation NI explained:

"The group was set up in response to disturbances that took place in the town several years ago. Since then, representatives of Comber and the Lithuanian community have been meeting monthly with us and Ards Borough Council to discuss how to improve relationships."

Andrius Cislikauskas, 25, moved to Northern Ireland at 18.

He runs a family restaurant in Comber and is a leading member of the Comber Diversity Project.

"I came to Northern Ireland to make a better life for myself. I was only 18 and didn't know what to expect but people here have treated me very well … After the riot in the town centre tensions started to increase between Lithuanians living in the town and local people. So when I was asked to get involved in the Comber Diversity Project I agreed as I felt it was important to find a solution that would help stop the tension that was developing on both sides … The main thing we were able to do was stop rumours on both sides getting out of control, which could lead to violence."

Crawford Perry, 50, founder member of Comber Residents Association.

He explains how he got involved in the Comber Diversity Project and how it has changed his views of his eastern European neighbours.

"I didn't really know very much about Lithuanians before I went on the residential with the project … This project has been very successful in bringing both sets of people together. A bond has definitely developed between us and it's all down to the fact that we have been able to learn more about each other's culture … There's definitely a greater understanding between us and people on both sides are no longer wary."

Text and images are both courtesy of *Big Lottery Fund's BIG magazine*, N.Ireland Issue 3, http://www2.biglotteryfund.org.uk/downloads/bigmag-ni3.pdf
For the full story visit: www.mediationnorthernireland.org

CHECK YOUR LEARNING

1. Explain how conflicts might arise between people from different ethnic backgrounds.

2. Explain how the Comber Diversity Project dealt with conflict between local residents and immigrants.

3. Why was mediation an important part of the whole process?

ACTION WITHOUT VIOLENCE

Conflict resolution is a creative approach to problem-solving in the local community, and it can also be effective on a global level if there are disputes to be resolved between nations. While violence offers a **destructive** response to conflict, conflict resolution is **constructive**.

Here are some ways the global community can put pressure on groups or governments to end conflict:

Judicial System

If a person feels that an injustice or criminal action has taken place towards them, then they should not take the law into their own hands. The matter should be reported to the police and then dealt with through the law courts.

Sanctions

A sanction is an official action taken against a country to force it to obey international law. A sanction usually involves stopping trade, so the country cannot import any goods or sell its exports. Over a period of time, this will seriously damage a county's economy, so the leaders of the country will agree to act reasonably so the sanctions can be lifted.

Boycotts

A boycott means a complete refusal to buy a product or take part in an activity as a way of registering a protest. In the past, some countries have boycotted the Olympic Games as a way of showing their disapproval of another country's actions. The biggest Olympic boycott ever was in 1980 when the games were held in Russia. A total of 61 countries did not compete in protest over the Russian invasion of Afghanistan.

International Human Rights Instruments

These can be divided into two categories:

- Declarations (which are not legally binding)
- Conventions (these are legally binding)

An example of a declaration is **The Declaration on the Rights of the Child**, and it describes how children ought to be treated. An example of a convention is

The **European Convention on Human Rights.** This protects human rights and basic freedom in Europe. Any person who feels that their rights are being denied can take their case to The European Court of Human Rights.

The United Nations Security Council Chamber, New York

The United Nations

The United Nations was founded in 1945 after the Second World War. It aims to maintain international peace, develop friendly relations among nations and promote human rights. The United Nations also has a range of other functions, including disaster relief, encouraging sustainable development and protecting refugees.

Some people feel that the United Nations is in need of reform to make it more effective in today's world.

ACTIVITIES

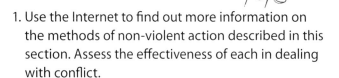

1. Use the Internet to find out more information on the methods of non-violent action described in this section. Assess the effectiveness of each in dealing with conflict.

2. Look at the Universal Declaration of Human Rights on page 46 of chapter two.

   Which rights are concerned with issues of diversity and exclusion?

evaluation

Evaluate the role of mediation as strategy for resolving conflict.

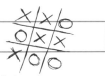
Consider the following situations and decide on a course of action from the list below:

- Sanctions
- Judicial action
- Mediation
- Boycott
- Violence

Situation 1

Hilda lives in a Housing Association flat. There have recently been a number of complaints that Hilda's behaviour is starting to upset the other residents and the Housing Association says that she has to leave. Her doctor believes that dementia is the cause of this and he recommends that a nursing home might give Hilda the care she needs. Hilda refuses to leave her flat.

How should the conflict be resolved?

Situation 2

Jim is a builder and he has to park his large van overnight in his driveway. New neighbours have recently moved in next door and they are constantly complaining that the van is spoiling their view. Jim has tried to ignore them rather than get into an argument. One morning, he discovers that the headlamps have been smashed on his van. The man across the street says he saw Jim's neighbour on his driveway late the previous night.

What should Jim do?

Situation 3

In 1955, in the American town of Montgomery, a black lady called Rosa Parks was ordered to give up her seat on a bus to a white man. The action that followed started out as a campaign against the seating on the buses but developed into a nation-wide civil rights movement, led by Martin Luther King.

What course of action was originally taken in this historical example? Was it successful?

Situation 4

From 1948 to 1994, South Africa had a policy called 'Apartheid'. It meant that black people and white people were kept separate, with black people having to endure appalling conditions in housing, healthcare and education. The United Nations condemned South Africa's policies and many countries throughout the world started to take action against South Africa.

How did the world community show disapproval of South Africa's actions? Was this action effective?

You could also...

- Write a possible outcome for each of the first two situations.
- Use the Internet to find out more about the two historical examples.

LIVING IN A MULTI-CULTURAL SOCIETY

In this section we will be considering some of the ways in which society can be made more inclusive. Although there are laws making discrimination illegal, it is attitudes that need to change. People's attitudes towards their neighbours, work colleagues and classmates from other cultural backgrounds are very important. A person may well feel far more included in society by an offer of friendship or small kindness, than by knowing that the law of the land is there to protect them. It is the responsibility of everyone to create a society where every citizen feels valued, equal and safe in the community. Cultural differences should not cause fear or discrimination, but cultural diversity can be celebrated as part of a vibrant society.

PROMOTING INCLUSION IN SCHOOLS

Schools can use a number of strategies to help everyone to feel they belong and where every child feels valued. If children can learn to be tolerant, then there is hope that in the future our society will become more inclusive. There are a number of legal obligations on schools to meet particular needs, for example, if a pupil has a disability. Some key ways for a school to promote inclusion are:

- **Language** – A pupil should not feel isolated because of language barriers and helping new arrivals to learn English should be a priority. If there are a significant number of pupils in the school from the same ethnic background, then it might be possible to have a translator in school, at least on a part-time basis. Some schools have a 'buddy' system where a pupil with the same first language can help a new arrival to settle in.

Parents should not be overlooked, as coping with letters home or parent-teacher meetings could be very stressful. An inclusive school could aim to have important school documents translated for parents who do not have English as a first language.

- **The curriculum** – A diversity calendar could be produced representing the religious traditions of all the pupils in the class. These festivals could be studied at the appropriate time of year as a way of encouraging inclusion. Younger pupils could listen to stories and sing songs from the various ethnic traditions represented by their classmates. The school curriculum could also cover human rights and issues relating to diversity and inclusion.

- **Anti-bullying policy** – Many families from ethnic minorities are affected by hate crime in their local community. Children can find themselves victims of racist bullying at school. A school should have an effective anti-bullying policy which specifically deals with racist behaviour in school as well as other forms of bullying.

INCLUSION IN THE WORKPLACE

Raising awareness of equality issues and making sure that employees know their rights are important in the workplace. Discrimination in the workplace is illegal; every employee has to have equal opportunity for employment, promotion, holidays, etc. However, people need to be made aware of the relevant legislation and their rights as employees. They can then ensure that they are being treated fairly and treat others in the same way.

The **Equality Commission for Northern Ireland** organises a number of campaigns throughout the year to raise public awareness on discrimination issues. It works in partnership with employers, trade unions and ethnic minority groups to organise **Anti-Racist Workplace Week**, which is held annually in October.

The aims of the initiative are:

- To raise awareness around the role the workplace can play in challenging racism in the wider community

- To ensure employees are made aware of their rights in the workplace, and

- To encourage employers to … achieve equality … for both employees and customers.

Source: http: www.equalityni.org

A MORE INCLUSIVE COMMUNITY

Raising awareness of the need for equality and addressing attitudes are important in trying to create a more tolerant and inclusive community. Some people argue that harsher penalties for those found guilty of discrimination might be more effective.

Are fines and prison sentences the best way to tackle inequality, or is raising people's awareness a better approach?

DISCUSSION
What do you think is the best course of action for society to take against discrimination?

The Equality Commission for Northern Ireland

The Equality Commission for Northern Ireland is concerned with inclusion in the whole of society as well as the workplace. Here are examples of campaigns to raise awareness and inform people of the law.

• Traveller Focus Week
This annual event aims to raise public awareness of some of the issues faced by the Traveller community,

and promotes good relations by increasing people's understanding of Traveller culture. Art exhibitions and Fun Days accompany more serious discussions about education and healthcare. This is an important campaign. Although Travellers are given protection under the law, they are still one of the most disadvantaged groups in society.

• ACCESS FOR ALL – It's the law
From January 2010, disabled people have legal protection against discrimination when using transport, such as trains, buses, coaches, taxis and vehicle breakdown services. The Equality Commission ran an advertising campaign to promote the new regulations. The campaign included television adverts, billboards and magazine advertising.

Football

• Kick It Out
'Kick It Out' is the name of football's campaign to raise awareness about equality and inclusion. The brand name 'Let's Kick Racism out of Football' was launched in 1993, and Kick It Out was established in 1997.

Kick It Out aims to challenge discrimination and work for a positive change in attitudes. It does not just work through football clubs, but through schools and the community as well. Kick It Out is supported and funded through the game's governing bodies, such as the Premier League and the Professional Footballers Association (PFA).

One of Kick It Out's areas of concern is Asian players. Football is very popular with many young Asians throughout the UK, but Asian players are massively under-represented in professional football. A campaign was launched in 2005 to address this issue, called 'Asians Can Play Football'.

Kick It Out is not just concerned with racism, but with other forms of discrimination as well:

> "As long as a player does the business during 90 minutes, his sexual persuasion just doesn't come into it. I would rather be playing alongside the best player in the world who is gay than someone who's not good enough."
>
> **Curtis Davies, Aston Villa**

> "If disabled fans want to go and watch sport then it shouldn't be a hassle for them to go and do it, you should be able to support your team the same as everyone else."
>
> **Danny Mills, Former England full-back**

More information is available on the Kick It Out website: www.kickitout.org

• **Show Racism the Red Card**

'Show Racism the Red Card' is an anti-racist charity, established in 1996. This organisation aims to combat racism through the use of high-profile footballers and educational resources. The sporting personalities involved with the charity are good role models who present an anti-racist message young people can relate to.

More information is available on the Show Racism the Red Card website: http://www.srtrc.org/

Samuel Eto'o

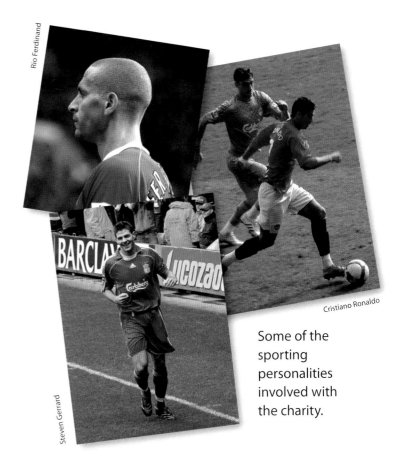

Rio Ferdinand

Steven Gerrard

Cristiano Ronaldo

Some of the sporting personalities involved with the charity.

RESEARCH ACTIVITY

Visit the websites of the charities discussed and find out more about campaigns to get rid of racism in sport:

Show Racism the Red Card – http://www.srtrc.org
Kick It Out – http://www.kickitout.org

CHECK YOUR LEARNING

1. Northern Ireland is now a multicultural society, with people from a diverse range of ethnic backgrounds. What qualities do you consider to be important in order for us to live together without misunderstanding, conflict and violence? Make a list of bullet points.

2. Write a paragraph to explain how ethnic minority groups can help to promote a more inclusive society. There are examples in this chapter. You could add to this using your own knowledge and experience or by Internet research.

QUIZ: HOW WELL DO YOU KNOW YOUR NEIGHBOURS

Are you up-to-date when it comes to cultural awareness? Try this quiz to see if you are well-informed ...

1. Which of these 3 is the largest ethnic minority currently living in Northern Ireland?

    A. Latin American

    B. Indian

    C. Polish

2. Which minority religious group has lived in Northern Ireland the longest?

    A. Bahá'í

    B. Jewish

    C. Hindu

3. How many different religions are practiced in Northern Ireland?

    A. 2

    B. Between 3 and 9

    C. More than 10

4. Which of the following is the most serious issue among ethnic minority groups in Northern Ireland?

    A. Being the victim of hate crime

    B. Trying to claim benefits

    C. Getting the rest of their family into the country

5. Which of these 3 racial groups has lived in Northern Ireland the longest?

    A. Portuguese

    B. Chinese

    C. Filipino

6. How many different languages are currently spoken by people living in Northern Ireland?

    A. Less than 20

    B. Around 50–60

    C. More than 100

7. Which ethnic minority group has the highest proportion of children less than 15 years of age?

    A. Polish

    B. Traveller

    C. Eastern orthodox Christians

8. Which of these 3 ethnic minority groups are least likely to receive any education, often due to prejudice and discrimination?

    A. Chinese

    B. Indian

    C. Traveller

9. The Hindu community regularly organises celebrations at which everyone is welcome.

    A. True

    B. False

10. Most people see Northern Ireland as a friendly and tolerant place in which to live.

    A. True

    B. False

ANSWERS

1. **C. Polish.**
2. **B. Jewish** – Historical records suggest that there have been Jews in Belfast since the seventeenth century.
3. **C. At least 10** (Bahá'í, Buddhism, Christianity, Hinduism, Islam, Judaism and Sikhism all have significant communities here and there are a number of smaller religious groups represented).
4. **A. Hate Crime** – This is one of the major issues currently dealt with by NICEM (Northern Ireland Council for Ethnic Minorities).
5. **B. Chinese** – Many families had settled in Belfast and established businesses by the 1960s.
6. **C. More than 100**
7. **B. Traveller** – Young people under the age of 15 represent around 50% of the Traveller population; approximately 40% are children under 10 years of age.
8. **C. Traveller** – Children from the traveller community often feel unwelcome in local schools, as people in the 'settled' community may have negative attitudes towards them.
9. **A. True** – The Hindu community organises Holi celebrations in the Spring and a Summer Mela; both are held in Belfast and everyone is welcome.
10. **A. True** – Most people here are friendly and tolerant toward those of different ethnic origins or religious background. However, there is a small minority here making people's lives miserable through hate crime.

What did you score?

If you scored at least 7 then you are up-to-date and well informed about cultural diversity issues.

If not, perhaps you should consider finding out a little bit more about the place where you live and the people who share it with you!

EXAM FOCUS

This section will appear at the end of every chapter. It will help you to develop your exam skills.

As well as covering different topics, your exam will also have different types of question testing different skills. One of these skills is to **demonstrate your knowledge and understanding.**

The following question tests this skill:

(a) Name **two** ways in which a person can express their cultural identity.

[2 marks]

(b) Identify and explain **two** ways in which Northern Ireland is becoming more culturally diverse. [4 marks]

(c) Identify and explain **two** ways in which a conflict between two communities might be resolved. [4 marks]

Question taken from CCEA's GCSE Learning for Life and Work Modular Specimen Assessment Materials, Unit 3: Local and Global Citizenship Specimen Paper (2009)

When answering part (b) and part (c) of this question, start by clearly stating what you are going to write about, then give your explanation.

You could begin part (b) in the following way:

"Awareness of festivals from different cultures: In Belfast, everyone can join in with Holi, a Hindu Festival. Some communities have special celebrations for Chinese New Year. In schools, pupils learn about World Religions and some of the celebrations associated with different faiths."

Continue this answer adding an example of your own.

Chapter two

RIGHTS AND RESPONSIBILITIES REGARDING LOCAL, NATIONAL AND GLOBAL ISSUES

CHAPTER SUMMARY

In this chapter you will be studying:

- **What it means to show social responsibility.**
- **Ways in which people can become more aware and active in local, national and global issues.**
- **The Universal Declaration of Human Rights.**
- **The balance between rights and responsibilities.**

SOCIAL RESPONSIBILITY

WHAT IS SOCIAL RESPONSIBILITY?

Do you notice if something is wrong? Does someone you know seem to be in difficulty or struggling to cope? Is there something in your local neighbourhood which needs to be put right? People who have social responsibility take notice and are prepared to do something.

Social responsibility could mean that you help support a charity, perhaps through volunteer work or donating money.

Taking responsibility for the community in which you live is very important, but it does not need to stop there. Many people believe in taking action, locally, nationally and globally. This could involve campaigning for laws to be changed, perhaps as part of a pressure group.

People who show social responsibility generally believe that everyone has a right to be protected and respected, and to live and work in a decent environment. Social responsibility involves having an awareness of what is going on around you within your:

- family
- circle of friends
- school
- local community
- country
- world

AN EXAMPLE FROM OUR COMMUNITY – 'BLACK SANTA'

There is a tradition at St Anne's Cathedral, Belfast that in the run-up to Christmas each year the Dean will 'Sit out' to raise money for charity. The tradition was started by Dean Sammy Crooks in 1976. The local press described him as Belfast's Black Santa because of the black clerical cloak that he wore as he stood outside with a small barrel for donations. Dean Crooks was followed by Dean Jack Shearer and Dean Houston McKelvey. By Christmas 2009, the Sit out had raised £6.2 million.

The community spirit and social awareness produced by the Sit outs is described by Belfast Cathedral on their website:

"The commencement of the Sit out attracts considerable attention in the local press, radio and television. The leaders of the four main Churches in Ireland, the Lord Mayor of Belfast and many other community leaders call at the Cathedral to greet the Dean ... and to contribute!

All the money gathered is donated to local charities with a proportion given to Christian Aid. The range of charities includes medical research; those caring for children, youth and the elderly; the improvement of employment opportunities for young people and a host of small charities which cannot afford paid fund-raisers.

Most of the money donated is given by people who come to the Cathedral during the Sit out. Contributions are made by individuals, families, schools, offices and workplaces.

Some schools send the collection from their Christmas Carol Services or the proceeds of their Christmas Shows.

Some school choirs and bands come and perform on the Cathedral steps during the Sit out. To the fore amongst the schools are the students of Fleming Fulton School who all cope daily with physical disability. The present Dean, Dr Houston McKelvey says 'These students exemplify the spirit of the Sit out. Despite the problems which they and their families cope with daily, they have an annual Pennies from Heaven appeal for the Sit out for which they collect coins in Coke bottles. They have raised thousands of pounds for the Sit out in this way'."'

For more information visit http://www.belfastcathedral.org/black-santa/

INTERNATIONAL CELEBRITIES

Some celebrities have a reputation for showing social responsibility. They will use their position of influence to highlight injustice or suffering and draw attention to these issues. As well as raising awareness, they often take part in programmes and activities to raise money for charities and organisations to help deal with the problem.

BONO
CAMPAIGNER AGAINST POVERTY

Bono, the lead singer of U2, has a long history of charity involvement, particularly for famine relief and poverty related issues.

He is associated with high profile music events involving large numbers of celebrities and huge amounts of money being raised. Bono was involved with the original Band Aid and Live Aid projects and helped Bob Geldof to organise Live 8 in 2005.

As well as being active in the fight against poverty and starvation, Bono has been involved in other charity work. In 2005, he helped to create EDUN, a company that specialises in fairly traded clothing, providing employment in developing countries. Bono has also given his support to AIDS charities working in Africa.

He has received three nominations for the Nobel Peace Prize and was knighted in 2007.

DAVID BECKHAM
GOODWILL AMBASSADOR TO UNICEF

UNICEF (the United Nations International Children's Fund) is the world's leading organisation focusing on children and their rights.

"David Beckham has supported UNICEF since his days at Manchester United. In July 2001, he travelled to Thailand with the team on their pre-season tour. There he visited the UNICEF-supported Kredtrakarn Centre, meeting children as young as five who had suffered exploitation at the hands of adults. In 2003, David, as part of the team, helped to launch the UNICEF UK 'End Child Exploitation' Campaign.

In January 2005, the former England football captain became a Goodwill Ambassador with a special focus on UNICEF's Sports for Development programme. David's first job as Ambassador was a visit to UNICEF's Supply Division in Copenhagen, to see for himself the crucial work being done to aid 1.5 million children affected by the tsunami in South Asia. David then launched a global appeal to raise funds to support UNICEF's urgent humanitarian work in the region.

David has pledged his support for the current 'Unite for Children, Unite against AIDS' campaign and has taken part in a series of films to promote the campaign's messages. He also captained 'Team UNICEF' in a special short film produced in association with MTV and FIFA. Featuring some of the World's top football players, the film highlighted UNICEF's 2006 FIFA World Cup theme 'Unite for Children, Unite for Peace'."

Source: 'David Beckham, Goodwill Ambassador', http://www.unicef.org.uk/celebrity/celebrity_biography.asp?celeb_id=27

RONAN KEATING
SUPPORTER OF CANCER CHARITIES

After his mother died of breast cancer in 1998, Ronan Keating's family set up the Marie Keating Foundation in her memory. The overall aim of the Foundation is to make cancer less frightening. The charity provides information on breast cancer free of charge through mobile information units. To raise funds for the project, Ronan has completed two sponsored walks across Ireland.

In 2009, Ronan received a Special Achievement Award from Cancer Research UK. Since 2006, he has raised over £1.7 million for this charity which is now linked to the Marie Keating Foundation.

Ronan Keating also has a long-term commitment to supporting Comic Relief, the UK charity which strives to create a just world free from poverty. In 1999, Boyzone released the fundraising single for Comic Relief. The band's version of 'When the going gets tough' reached number one in the UK singles charts, with all the profits going to charity. More recently, Ronan's commitment to Comic Relief was shown when he joined a team of celebrities in 2009 to climb Mount Kilimanjaro in Africa. All nine celebrities reached the summit and raised over three million pounds for Comic Relief.

Ronan Keating's other charity involvement includes visiting Africa in 2004 as an ambassador for Christian Aid. He also preformed in the 2005 Live 8 concert.

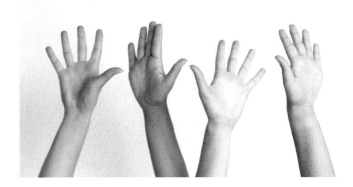

DISCUSSION

- Do you think it is a good thing for celebrities to show social responsibility and become involved in charity work?

- Why do you think many charities are pleased to be identified with celebrities?

- Read the following dialogue:

KEVIN: Celebrities really annoy me. They make a big deal of supporting charities, but if they really wanted to help, they would give away all their millions and live like ordinary people.

LOUISE: Why should they? They are entitled to their money; after all, they have earned it!

KEVIN: Sometimes I think they just get behind a good cause for all the publicity they will get out of it.

LOUISE: So, what is wrong with that? You've got to admit that celebrities do a lot of good and raise a huge amount for charity.

- Which point of view do you agree with?

- Organise a class debate with the motion *"This house believes that celebrities are more concerned with their own publicity than helping good causes."* You need to have two people to speak FOR the motion and two people to speak AGAINST it, with a chair person to keep order!

WHY VOLUNTEER?

Some people might wonder what the point is of doing voluntary work. After all, surely work is either something you should get paid for, or you only do it because you have to? There are many reasons for volunteering and many benefits that it can bring to both the community and the individual involved.

One of the unique features of volunteering is that it can give you a completely different outlook. You are working at something simply because you want to, or because you believe that what you are doing is worthwhile. Working for a sense of satisfaction, rather than money, means you are not so likely to be watching the clock and waiting for the time to finish work. Volunteers can have a lot of fun, and make new friends, while doing valuable work at the same time. This might involve working in a charity shop, organising a children's party or talking on the phone to a person who is upset. There are many opportunities to get involved in voluntary work!

THE BENEFITS OF VOLUNTEERING

Volunteering can make a real difference to individuals, the local community and the environment. Many charities and Non-Governmental Organisations (NGOs) rely on volunteer help; they simply do not have the funds to pay all their workers. Using volunteers means that more money can be spent on carrying out their work.

Some of the groups that rely on volunteering play an important role in looking after the environment or local facilities, so the whole community can benefit from voluntary work. There may be neighbourhood schemes to help elderly people with gardening and minor household repairs, or to clear up a piece of waste land for a children's play area.

However, some of the greatest benefits from volunteering are for the volunteer. Here are some examples:

- **An opportunity to meet people and make new friends:** People of all ages and from all walks of life get involved in voluntary work, so it is a great way to get to know people from different backgrounds. However, you will probably have something in common – a commitment to the work you are doing and the belief that it is worthwhile.

- **A chance to gain some valuable work experience:** Possible employers may look at previous voluntary work as showing a high level of commitment by the volunteer. If you are considering a particular career for the future, then volunteering in that area might help you decide if it really is for you.

- **The satisfaction of knowing you are doing something worthwhile:** Voluntary work often involves helping others, and can give a person a feeling of satisfaction and 'giving something back'. Perhaps a person has struggled with a particular issue themselves and wants to help others in a similar situation. Someone who has come to terms with an addiction problem might volunteer to give counselling to others with the same addiction, for example.

- **A boost to self-confidence**: Voluntary work can provide the opportunity to develop new skills or attain a personal goal. An office manager might really want to work with young people, so volunteering to help out at the local youth club might be a way of achieving this. Working as part of a team, and knowing that your contribution is important can help to improve your self-esteem.

- **A greater involvement in the local community:** A family who has recently moved into an area might find that voluntary work can give them a sense of belonging. Helping out at a nearby charity shop, or becoming involved with a local residents' association can help a person to feel part of their community, and that their contribution is valued.

As one young person commented…

"Volunteering is an experience that benefits me greatly in every aspect of day to day life, qualities I learn such as confidence, being a good team player, self-esteem, being able to address a group of people. It is enjoyable, worthwhile and I just love it!"

Source: VSB, http://www.vsb.org.uk/ycia/

CASE STUDY: HABITAT FOR HUMANITY

Habitat for Humanity is a Christian NGO working with communities in Northern Ireland and worldwide. Volunteers are central to their work.

"Habitat for Humanity is committed to the vision of a world where everyone has a decent place to live. Since its founding in 1976, Habitat has built more than 300,000 houses worldwide, providing simple, decent and affordable shelter for more than 1.5 million people in over 90 countries.

Habitat for Humanity Northern Ireland was founded in 1994; the work is focused on regenerating and reconciling communities that have suffered from 35 years of conflict and on delivering affordable housing solutions in areas most at risk. For 15 years self-build home ownership projects have brought together more than 10,000 volunteers from both traditions to build alongside families in need in both Protestant and Catholic interface communities.

These projects have helped to regenerate communities and restore relationships by building over 85 houses across 7 communities in West and North Belfast, Downpatrick and Omagh. New projects are being developed in other areas impacted by deprivation and the legacy of conflict.

For every house built locally we fund and build 10 houses internationally.

Habitat for Humanity Northern Ireland is a key partner in Habitat's global mission; raising funds to support international projects and advocating on behalf of those in need of decent shelter.

Through the Global Village Programme Habitat for Humanity Northern Ireland provides opportunities for local volunteers and teams from all backgrounds and across the sectarian divide, to work in communities in need around the world, building houses.

1 in 1,000 people from Northern Ireland have travelled on almost 200 Global Village teams to build homes in some 32 countries worldwide. Many of these projects are in conflict or post conflict communities similar to Northern Ireland.

Volunteers are central to Habitat's work both locally and globally. During 2009 we brought together more than 2000 volunteers on-site through a range of opportunities designed to challenge those who participate and deepen the impact for individuals and communities."

For more information visit:
www.habitatni.co.uk

CHECK YOUR UNDERSTANDING

1. Explain how volunteering is central to the work of Habitat for Humanity.
2. How does Habitat for Humanity encourage social responsibility both at home and overseas?

Some important considerations…
For a person contemplating voluntary work there are some important questions to be considered:

What type of work do I want to do?
What issues do you feel strongly about? Are you concerned about the environment or human rights? Would you like to help children or elderly people? Would practical, outdoor work be best or something sitting down inside? It is important to think carefully about the type of work that would suit you best and what you would enjoy doing.

How much time can I give?
Even though the work is unpaid, people still rely on volunteer workers. It is therefore important to be dependable and not to make a commitment you cannot keep to. The volunteer football coach needs to turn up every time the youth club team has a practice!

What skills do I have to offer?
Some people might have skills that could be put to good use, such as typing or gardening. Others may be suited to hospital visiting or befriending an elderly person. However, many volunteers simply offer an enthusiasm to get involved and a willingness to work with others.

ACTIVITY

Work in groups of about four or five.

- Decide on a project for a local area that you are familiar with. The aim of this project is to improve the area and to benefit the lives of local residents.
- In planning your project, try to include ways to involve the whole community.
- Share your ideas with the rest of the class as a PowerPoint presentation.

CASE STUDY: TIDY NORTHERN IRELAND

TIDY Northern Ireland is a local environmental NGO. It seeks to encourage social responsibility and relies mainly on volunteers.

"We produce information on the cleanliness of our province that is used to direct resources to tackle the most prominent environmental quality issues. TIDY NI is best known for its campaigns and public information on litter including car litter, gum deposition, drugs related litter, fast food litter and youth litter. However, we have also

campaigned on a number of other anti-social behaviour issues such as fly-tipping, dog fouling and neighbourhood noise.

TIDY NI endorses the government's wider aim to deliver sustainable development. This work falls into three main areas: campaigning to get public action, the delivery of programmes to enable partners to deliver action in the community and the production of research and survey results to measure the quality of the local environment."

The vision for TIDY Northern Ireland is to be one of the leading organisations working for a better environment. This gives local people a greater sense of responsibility, so problems such as anti-social behaviour and litter will be reduced.

For more information visit:
http://www.tidynorthernireland.org

CHECK YOUR UNDERSTANDING

1. Explain how TIDY NI can encourage people to take responsibility for their local community.
2. What are some of the main issues that TIDY NI is concerned with?

ACTIVITY

ANYONE CAN VOLUNTEER!

Use the Internet to find suitable voluntary work for each of the following people:

Margaret is a fit and active 72 year old. She loves to get out of the house and meet people, but since her husband's illness and death last year, she has been feeling particularly lonely. Margaret would love to do something to support her local hospice, which gave her a lot of support when her husband was ill.

What volunteering opportunities would be suitable for Margaret?

If there is one thing that makes Nathan really annoyed, its people who treat the local environment as a rubbish dump! He lives in the country where he sees rubbish dumped in hedgerows and along the banks of a local river. Nathan is 38 years old and self-employed as a builder, so his working hours are fairly flexible.

What opportunities are there for Nathan to get involved with local environmental issues and also do something practical?

Anna is 17 years old and has just finished her AS exams. She is hoping to go to college when she finishes school and train as a primary school teacher as she loves working with children.

What voluntary work could Anna do during her summer holidays? She would like to have fun and also gain some valuable work experience.

Evaluate how voluntary work can benefit both the volunteer and the community.

TAKING ACTION: PRESSURE GROUPS

WHAT IS A PRESSURE GROUP?

A **pressure group** is an organised group of people who aim to influence government policy, or the laws that they pass. Pressure groups do not offer candidates for election or look for power for themselves – they just seek to influence those who do hold political power. There are a large number of pressure groups in the UK. Here are some examples:

- **British Union for the Abolition of Vivisection** – Seeking to bring an end to the use of animals in experiments.
- **Earth First** – Campaigning against the destruction of the environment.
- **National Union of Students (NUS)** – Seeking to draw attention to issues concerning students and bring their needs to the government.
- **Shelter** – Taking action against homelessness and poor housing.
- **National Society for the Prevention of Cruelty to Children (NSPCC)** – Campaigning to end all abuse of children.

Some groups are known as **sectional pressure groups**, as they represent the interests of a particular section of society (for example the NUS). Others are known as **cause pressure groups** because they represent a cause that everyone could be interested in (for example Earth First).

PRESSURE GROUP STRATEGIES

A pressure group is only effective if it can have an influence on the government. To do this, the group has to be noticed and it must put its message across effectively. There are a variety of ways in which pressure groups try to achieve this and most of these methods are regarded as ethical and within the law. However, not all pressure groups act within the law. There are some militant and extremist pressure groups that will harm human life or property in order to make their cause known.

Here are some of the main strategies used by pressure groups:

- **Lobbying MPs:** This is a system of persuasion used by some pressure groups and it involves convincing a member of parliament that changes need to be made in a certain area.

- **Writing to a local councillor or newspaper:** This can be an effective way of publicising a campaign and attempting to get others to agree.

- **A march or demonstration:** For maximum effectiveness, this type of protest might be timed to coincide with a crucial meeting that is taking place. Sometimes a march or demonstration will focus on a particular building; for example, pro-life demonstrators may protest outside an abortion clinic.

- **Petition:** Collecting signatures is a way of showing the decision-makers just how many people you have on your side, and this can be very effective.

- **Use of celebrities:** Public support is important for pressure groups as the government is then more likely to take notice of them. Many people are more likely to support a cause if it is promoted by a celebrity they admire.

- **Propaganda:** This is a way of presenting information to the public in order to make people agree with you. Propaganda does not actually involve telling direct lies, but sometimes it can be very misleading. Certain facts can be left out and information distorted to give a false impression. For example, a pressure group might try to scare people with misleading information about climate change or the quality of our water supply.

- **Publicity stunt:** This is a planned event, aimed at getting the attention of both the general public and the media. Publicity stunts can involve celebrities, a dangerous challenge or an act of protest. In the past, environmental campaigners have chained themselves to trees about to be cut down to make way for new roads.

- **Use of violence or criminal activity:** These tactics are only used by a small minority of pressure groups. Some protestors maintain that damage to property can be justified, such as setting fire to a laboratory that uses animals in experiments. A very small minority believe they can justify threats to human life to further their cause.

CASE STUDY: THE NORTHERN IRELAND YOUTH FORUM (NIYF)

The Northern Ireland Youth Forum is a pressure group concerned with young people and the issues they face. It is active on both a local and national level.

"Ever wished that you could change the way your youth club is run? Or maybe re-write the bus schedule so that you didn't miss that bus which finished just after school time? Maybe you fancy yourself as a bit of a politician? Or you just want to tell someone what you think about the park in your area?

NIYF is all about young people being included in decision-making, and having their voice heard. You don't have to be super-human, or an amazing speechwriter, you just have to have something to say – NIYF is here to help you.

There are a number of ways in which you can get involved in NIYF, from as small as receiving an email newsletter every month to as big as becoming a member of our Executive Committee which runs the organisation.

The Northern Ireland Youth Forum (NIYF) is run by young people and is all about young people. Any young person (11–25) can get involved.

We were set up 30 years ago to represent the views of young people in Northern Ireland to government and other decision makers.

We believe that ALL young people have ideas and opinions worth listening to and we want to help you get involved in changing things in your school, community, home and in government.

The NIYF is a youth led organisation that lobbies, advocates, promotes and fights for the rights of young people in NI. We aim to build the confidence and awareness of all young people so that they can assert their rights."

For more information visit: http://www.niyf.org

CHECK YOUR UNDERSTANDING

1. Explain how young people can get involved with the NIYF.

2. What are the aims of this organisation?

BE AN ACTIVE CITIZEN …

… in your school, local community and globally. How?

Visit the following website to find out more:

http://www.bbc.co.uk/schools/citizenx/local/community/act.shtml

Try the **Pantz Park** activity and take action to fix up a vandalised area.

DIRECT AND INDIRECT ACTION

Some pressure groups use **direct action** to prove their point. This includes groups that resort to violence, but direct action is not necessarily violent or aggressive.

Historically, non-violent actions are more effective. Martin Luther King Jr used non-violent action to win civil rights for African-Americans in the 1960s. Mahatma Gandhi ended British rule in India without using violence. Examples of direct action include:

- **sit-ins and marches** – where large groups of people gather to draw attention to an issue.

- **strikes** – where people refuse to do their jobs, possibly to convince their employers to improve their pay or conditions.

- **civil disobedience** – where someone deliberately disobeys the government or breaks a law because they believe it is unjust. This may result in arrest.

Most pressure groups use **indirect action**. This can include writing letters to MPs and decision-makers, gathering petitions, and raising awareness in order to gain public support.

Many successful campaigns use direct and indirect action working together to bring results. Indirect action often works in the background to support direct action, while direct action can add force to indirect action.

ACTIVITY

Make a copy of the table below.

- Consider the advantages and disadvantages for each pressure group strategy.
- Rate each strategy between 1–10 according to how effective you think it is, with '1' being the **most** effective.

DISCUSSION

- Is it ever right for a pressure group to use violence to further their cause?
- What is the difference between violence against property and violence against a person?
- *"A pressure group will only be effective if it has the support of the general public."*
  Do you agree or disagree? Give reasons for your view.

STRATEGY	ADVANTAGES	DISADVANTAGES	RATING
Lobbying an MP			
Writing to local councillor/ newspaper			
March/demonstration			
Petition			
Celebrities			
Propaganda			
Publicity stunt			
Violence/criminal activity			

HUMAN RIGHTS

WHY DO WE NEED HUMAN RIGHTS?

Human Rights are defined as *"The basic rights and freedoms to which all humans are entitled"*. Some rights are concerned with physical needs, such as decent housing and health care. Others refer to the right of each citizen to have their own opinions and follow a religion if they choose to. Human rights are a basic guarantee that each person can have decent standard of living.

The need to be aware of human rights is vitally important. Many people in the world live in poverty, without access to clean water, adequate food or health care; others are tortured or imprisoned without trial because their government does not agree with their opinions. In our society, there are people who face discrimination because of their gender, ethnic origins or sexual orientation. We need human rights to ensure the fair and equal treatment of every citizen.

Human rights are all about people … the little girl working long hours in the carpet factory in India, because her small hands and keen eyesight are suited to the delicate work … the worker on the banana plantation in Ecuador, who is paid so little he can barely feed his family … the confused, elderly person in a nursing home in Northern Ireland who is told to 'behave' or her grandchildren will not be allowed to visit her. These are examples of some of the human rights issues that will be covered in this section.

A SHORT HISTORY OF HUMAN RIGHTS

The term 'Human Rights' came into use in the twentieth century, but the idea of having fair and equal treatment for everyone is not new.

Plato and Aristotle by Raffaello Sanzio

- In the fourth century BCE, the Greek philosophers **Plato** and **Aristotle** put forward their ideas of justice. They believed that some people had a lower position in society than others – slaves, for example – but everyone with the same status has to be treated with equality.

- In the sixth century CE, a Roman called **Justinian** produced rules for the benefit of everyone in society. These laws established the idea that every citizen has rights and duties, so they were a step in the right direction towards human rights.

- In 1215 **King John** was forced to sign a document called the **Magna Carta.** This guaranteed rights to rich landowners, not to every citizen. However, it was the first time in history that laws in the British Isles had tried to protect rights.

- In the seventeenth century some thinkers developed the idea that people had rights simply because they were human. These rights were called **'natural rights'** or **'the rights of man'.** Philosopher Thomas Hobbes (1588–1679) argued that it was the government's duty to protect everyone in society. Politician and philosopher John Locke (1632–1704) believed that people had the right to freedom of speech, the right to worship and the right to own property. Thinkers such as these had a significant impact on people's views about rights.

- **The American Declaration of Independence** was produced in 1776. It established that all men were created equal and had certain rights, such as *"Life, Liberty and the pursuit of happiness"*. The government had a duty to protect these rights.

- In 1833, William Wilberforce was successful in his campaign to **abolish slavery** in Britain and its colonies.

- After the suffering of the Second World War, many people realised there was a need to protect human rights. In 1948 the **Universal Declaration of Human Rights** (UDHR) was produced by the United Nations. It consists of 30 articles and describes the rights which all human beings are entitled to, wherever they live. Countries sign up to the UDHR to show their intention to protect the rights of their citizens and it has become the standard against which human dignity and quality of life are measured.

- In 1961, the human rights organisation **Amnesty International** was founded.

- Other documents have been produced by the UN to ensure that human rights are respected. In 1966 two international covenants were produced, one concerning civil and political rights and the other economic, social and cultural rights. Together with the UDHR, these make up the **International Bill of Human Rights** which came into force in 1976.

ACTIVITY

Produce a timeline of the important events in the history of human rights.

THE UNIVERSAL DECLARATION OF HUMAN RIGHTS
(a summary)

1. Everyone is born free and equal.
2. Everyone is entitled to all rights, regardless of their skin colour, sex, religion, language, etc.
3. Everyone has the right to life and to live in freedom and safety.
4. No one should be treated as a slave.
5. No one has the right to hurt you or to torture you.
6. Everyone has the right to fair treatment by the law of every country.
7. The law is the same for everyone, it should be applied in the same way to all.
8. Everyone has the right to ask for legal help when their rights are not respected.
9. No one should be imprisoned or expelled from their own country without a fair trial.
10. Everyone has the right to a fair and public trial.
11. Everyone should be considered innocent until guilt is proved.
12. Everyone has the right to ask for help if someone tries to harm you. No-one can enter your home, open your letters or bother you or your family without a good reason.
13. Everyone has the right to travel as they wish.
14. Everyone has the right to go to another country and ask for protection if they are being persecuted or are in danger of being persecuted.
15. Everyone has the right to belong to a country. No one has the right to prevent you from belonging to another country if you wish to.
16. Everyone has the right to marry and have a family. Families should be protected by the government.
17. Everyone has the right to own property and possessions.
18. Everyone has the right to practise and observe all aspects of their own religion and change their religion if they want to.
19. Everyone has the right to say what they think and to give and receive information.
20. Everyone has the right to take part in meetings and to join associations in a peaceful way.
21. Everyone has the right to help choose and take part in the government of their country.
22. Everyone has the right to social security and to opportunities to develop their skills.
23. Everyone has the right to work for a fair wage in a safe environment and to join a trade union.
24. Everyone has the right to rest and leisure.
25. Everyone has the right to an adequate standard of living and medical help if they have no income because of unemployment, illness, disability, old age, or the death of a spouse.
26. Everyone has the right to an education.
27. Everyone has the right to share in their community's cultural life.
28. Everyone must respect the 'social order' that is necessary for all these rights to be available.
29. Everyone must respect the rights of others, the community and public property.
30. No one has the right to take away any of the rights in this declaration.

Source: http://web.amnesty.org/pages/hre-first-eng

DISCUSSION

Think about these questions, and then discuss them with others in the class:

- Why it is it important that everyone should have human rights?

- Can you think of any people in society who should not have any of these rights?

- Can human rights change depending on the circumstances?

- Are some rights more important than others?
- Why do different cultures and countries have different ideas about human rights? Can you think of examples?
- If a country is ignoring human rights, should other countries intervene?
- Can you think of any examples, in the local community and worldwide, where human rights are being ignored?

FOCUS ON SOME IMPORTANT RIGHTS FROM THE UDHR

Everyone has the right to life and to live in freedom and safety. (Article 3)

Having the right to life is the most basic and important right that a person can have. However, it can also be one of the most controversial. For example, some people are in favour of the death penalty. They believe that if someone takes the life of another then they forfeit their right to life and the state is justified in putting them to death. Abortion is another controversial issue. Does the right to life include unborn babies in the womb? Those who are in favour of abortion would argue that a foetus does not necessarily have the right to life.

Most people would agree that every human being, regardless of their race, religion, sexuality, social class or political beliefs has the right to life – and to live in freedom and safety. It is the responsibility of local and national governments to provide safety and security in society for all citizens. The police and the courts can do this through the laws that are made and the way they are enforced. An effective legal system is one that protects people but does not deny anyone their basic right of freedom.

Read the examples which follow. In what way does each one show this right being abused?

- **Genocide** is the attempt to systematically wipe out an entire race of people, denying them

their right to life and to live in safety. A historical example of this is **The Holocaust**, the Nazi's attempt to exterminate Jewish people in the death camps of the Second World War. As a result of this, over six million Jews were killed.

- Despite this atrocity, genocide has continued. In 1994, the African country of **Rwanda** experienced some dreadful human rights abuses. There are two ethnic groups in Rwanda, the majority Hutu and the much smaller Tutsi population. When tensions between these groups flared into violence, at least half a million people were massacred in genocide, about three quarters of the Tutsi population.

- Prejudice towards Jewish people did not end with The Holocaust. **The Community Security Trust** is a charity that monitors anti-semitism in Britain today. In 2009 they reported a significant increase in hate crimes towards Jewish people. In one incident, a man left his local synagogue driving an electric wheelchair. He was rammed by a car as the driver shouted "Jew" at him, but luckily he was not seriously injured.

Everyone has the right to ask for help if someone tries to harm you, no-one can enter your home, open your letters or bother you or your family without a good reason. (Article 12)

Everyone has the right to privacy, which means a person has the right to live their life without being pestered or spied on. If someone feels that they are being denied this right, then they are entitled to protection from the law. However, the phrase 'without good reason' suggests that there may be circumstances where this right does not have to be respected. It would be routine practice for prisoners to have their letters opened and checked before they receive them. If the police suspect someone of a crime they can obtain permission from the courts to record telephone conversations. Most people would consider these practices necessary for security rather than a denial of human rights.

However, when the media intrudes into a person's privacy, this is a more controversial issue. Some people feel this is the price that celebrities have to pay for their fame and luxurious lifestyles. If a politician is involved in a scandal then every detail might appear in the press as it is seen to be in the public's interest. An alternative view is that this is an unnecessary attack on a person's reputation and a denial of their rights.

Has this right been abused in the following examples?

- Police in Britain have the right to stop and search a vehicle if they have a 'reasonable suspicion' that it might be involved in a crime. They can also stop and search a person for weapons or drugs. A house or business cannot be searched without a warrant issued by a court of law. However, the law is different in Northern Ireland. Under section 44 of the Terrorism Act, the PSNI can stop and search vehicles and people in a designated area without any grounds for suspicion. A person can have their clothing or possessions searched on the street. Some politicians claim the PSNI no longer need these special powers and that they should be withdrawn.

- In 1997, Diana Princess of Wales died in a fatal car crash and this raised questions about the media and privacy. The term 'paparazzi' refers to freelance photographers who constantly pursue a celebrity or member of the Royal Family. At the inquest following the accident, the paparazzi chasing the Princess's car were found to be partly responsible for her death. Her driver was also found to be at fault, as he had been drinking and was driving extremely fast.

Everyone has the right to help choose and take part in the government of their country. (Article 21)

A democracy is a form of government where the ordinary people can take part in the process of choosing who will rule them. If everyone has a vote, and people are free to vote as they choose, then the government that is elected will be the choice of the majority. A good democratic government will try to ensure that everybody is treated fairly, not just a privileged few. Everyone in society has the right to take part in the government of their country, either by choosing politicians to represent them or being elected themselves. Elections should be held regularly and a person must be able to vote in secret. All votes should be equal.

Even though people might complain about their government, it is an important human right to live in a democracy. If a dictator takes control, supported by military power, then this might lead to many other human rights abuses in that country. These could include imprisonment without trial and torture for anyone opposing the dictator.

What human rights have been denied in the following example?

- China is not a democracy. In April 1989, thousands of students and workers started to gather in **Tiananmen Square**, in Beijing. They demanded freedom for the press and a reform of the government. News reports in the UK and America described the demonstrators as 'pro-democratic' but in China they were seen as trouble-makers, intent on upsetting the government. The demonstrators did not use violence; they sang patriotic songs, listened to speeches and encouraged people to join the protest by going on strike. After seven weeks, the Chinese government took action to clear the square and they sent in troops and tanks. Most of the protestors were either shot or wounded. According to Western journalists reporting from Beijing, nearly 3,000 people were killed in the massacre. However, the official figure from the Chinese government is that it was less than 300.

Everyone has the right to work for a fair wage in a safe environment and to join a trade union.
(Article 23)

Everyone has the right to work, but this can be difficult in an area of high unemployment or in a very poor country. This problem requires a government to be committed to creating jobs. A government also has to make sure that wages are fair. Laws can be passed to ensure that there is a decent minimum wage and that everyone receives equal pay for equal work. A worker has the right to wages that will allow him or her to provide for their family.

Everyone has the right to work in a safe and comfortable environment. Employers have a duty to provide these conditions for their workers and the government should pass laws to ensure that this happens.

A **trade union** is an organised group of employees, usually involved in a similar line of work. The purpose of a trade union is to protect the working rights of its members. If a worker is in dispute with their employer over working conditions or pay, for example, then the trade union could speak on their behalf. This might

involve reminding the employer of their duties and warning them of legal consequences if they do not co-operate. It is the right of every worker to be in a trade union if they wish.

DISCUSSION

Should we only buy fairly traded bananas?
The banana industry has a very poor record for trade union rights. Most of the bananas in our shops come from large plantations in South America, employing poorly paid workers with very little job security. Ecuador is the world's largest banana producer, and although there are laws to protect workers and give them the right to join a trade union, these are often ignored. Banana workers can be dismissed for taking part in union activities, often because they are only given short-term contracts. Perhaps this is worth thinking about the next time you peel a banana!

FAIRTRADE

Many products we enjoy in the UK are grown in some of the world's less economically developed countries (LEDCs) in Africa, Asia and Latin America. These products include tea, coffee, cocoa, sugar, rice, cotton and different types of fruit. Often the farmers who grow these have small farms and suffer from unfair international trade rules that benefit richer countries. The processing and sale of these products is often controlled by a few very large companies who pay farmers little for their hard work, so they can lower the prices of the finished products. As a result many of these farmers fail to get a fair share of the financial benefits from this trade. The Fairtrade foundation seeks to address this by ensuring farmers are paid a fair and stable price, which covers the cost of sustainable production, and to establish long-term trading relationships. Companies also pay a Fairtrade Premium, which producers choose how to invest in their communities such as improving the way they farm to protect the environment, or building schools and hospitals. The FAIRTRADE Mark show shoppers all of this. Find out more at www.fairtrade.org.uk

® **Look for the Mark on Fairtrade products www.fairtrade.org.uk**

Do children have the right to work or the right to a childhood?

In the UK, young people have to be at least 14 years old before having a part-time job. However, in some parts of the world, children as young as 4 or 5 will work for many hours each day, just to help their family survive. In India, child labour is a very serious problem. Many young children work in factories making many different products, including carpets, fireworks and glass ware as their small hands are suited to delicate tasks. According to statistics from the Indian government, there are 20 million child labourers in the country, although this is probably a low estimate. On the other hand, some people say that if all child labour was banned, very poor families would suffer even greater hardship as they depend on their children's wages.

Everyone has the right to an adequate standard of living and medical help if they have no income because of unemployment, illness, disability, old age, or the death of a spouse. (Article 25)

It can be difficult to decide what is meant by an 'adequate standard of living' and this can vary according to where a person lives. However, all human beings have the right to decent food, clothing, housing and medical care. A person who is unable to work because of unemployment, disability, sickness or old age has the right to be provided for. Parenthood and childhood are also entitled to special assistance, and all children have the same rights regardless of whether or not their parents are married. The main purpose of this article is to try and stamp out poverty and ensure that all people everywhere have the right to live with dignity.

Which of the following examples do you consider to be the most shocking? Why?

- According to the United Nations, around 25,000 people die each day from starvation or hunger-related causes. The majority of these deaths will be children living in less developed countries. There is enough food in the world to feed everybody, but there is a serious problem of unfair distribution. Another problem is that people who are too poor to buy sufficient food for themselves and their family become malnourished. They then grow weak and sick, making it difficult to work and as a result become even poorer and hungrier. This is the downward spiral of poverty that can result in death.

- Starvation is not normally a problem in Northern Ireland. However, the children's charity Barnardos recently produced a report in which they claim 100,000 children are living in poverty in Northern Ireland. These children usually have a poor diet of low-quality food.

  Children living in disadvantaged areas in Northern Ireland are less likely to do well at school and have limited opportunities for employment. Disadvantaged homes may be unable to afford a washing machine, television or central heating. Children growing up in poverty are more likely to become parents during their teenage years.

  According to the Barnardos report, ethnic minority families, single-parent families and families with a disabled parent are more likely to find themselves living in poverty.

Information from: *'It doesn't happen here – The reality of child poverty in Northern Ireland, Barnardos Northern Ireland,* http://www.barnardos.org.uk/it_doesnt_happen_here_ni-2.pdf

Everyone has the right to an education.
(Article 26)

Everyone has the right to an education, which should be free and compulsory for childhood years. After this, technical and professional education should be generally available, and higher education equally accessible to everyone on the basis of merit. Parents have the right to choose how their children will be taught, and what they should learn.

Education is an important human right and it should also strengthen respect for human rights. At school, children should be taught to show respect for others, whatever their race, religion or nationality. Education should promote peace, tolerance and understanding.

Most governments are trying to increase their resources for education. There are still problems in some of the poorest countries of the world, where parents either cannot afford to pay for schooling or must send their children to work at a very young age. Some children cannot receive an education because of discrimination and racism.

DISCUSSION

What are the barriers to education in the following examples?

• *Afghanistan* has a very poor education record, with high rates of illiteracy and a low rate

of school attendance. Until 2001, the Taliban ruled Afghanistan. This was a strict Islamic group who banned the education of all females from primary school to university. Since the Taliban fell from power, more than a million girls are now attending school in Afghanistan. However, many people still remain hostile to the education of girls.

• It is widely recognised that children from the *Irish Traveller community*, both north and south of the border, face a range of barriers to their education. While this may be partly due to their lifestyle, it can also be caused by racism and intolerance in society. Many traveller young people reach the age of 16 with no formal qualifications and very poor literacy and numeracy skills. Action is now being taken to try and improve the educational prospects of children from this ethnic minority group.

CHILDREN'S RIGHTS

In 1990, the United Nations Convention on the Rights of the Child was produced. It recognises that children are particularly vulnerable and need special protection. It covers civil rights, health and welfare, education, family environment and leisure activities. Almost all countries in the world have agreed to adopt this convention.

However, throughout the world, not all children receive their rights. They are denied an education, forced to work or fight as soldiers, live on the streets or suffer cruelty at the hands of adults. Here are some issues that are causing particular concern:

• **Street children** – It is estimated that there are between 100 million and 150 million street children in the world. Children might be forced to live on the streets because their parents are too poor to provide for them, or because violence or abuse at home has forced them to run away. Street children are particularly vulnerable. They are unlikely to receive any education, will have a poor diet and little or no health care. Street children make a meagre living, perhaps through casual work or prostitution, but they are constantly at risk from violence or abuse. In some parts of the world, these homeless children are regarded as 'social vermin' and are routinely shot by the police in what is described as 'social cleansing'.

Some South American countries have a poor reputation for their treatment of street children, one example being Honduras. It is estimated that 7,500 children live on the streets and every year thousands die. Human rights organisations have put pressure on the Honduran government to bring the killers of street children to justice, but there have been very few prosecutions.

• **Child soldiers** – International law prohibits young people under the age of 18 taking part in armed conflict, and the use of children under the age of 15 is considered a war crime. However, throughout the world many thousands of children – some as young as 9 or 10 years old – are given weapons and forced to fight for the government armed forces or paramilitaries. Some children have witnessed their whole family being killed in conflict and see no alternative but to agree to fight. Child soldiers are frequently sent into the frontline of any fighting rather than have the lives of trained, adult soldiers put at risk. Children are also used as spies, messengers, porters and servants. Girls are particularly at risk of rape and sexual abuse.

• **Children accused of crimes** - Many people feel that the death penalty should be completely abolished for all offenders. However, there are still some countries in the world that put child offenders to death. Pakistan is one of these countries, where there are around

4,000 children in detention centres. More than 3,000 of these children are awaiting trial and have not yet been convicted of any offence.

• **Violence against children** – Throughout the world, children routinely face violence as part of their everyday lives, perhaps in school and often in their homes. Whether or not a child should be smacked by a parent or carer is a controversial issue in the UK. In 2004, there was a debate in the House of Commons about a complete ban on parents smacking their children. The ban was rejected as most MPs thought parents had a right to discipline their children through 'moderate smacking'.

DISCUSSION

1. **Do you think parents/carers should be allowed to smack their children?**

2. **Is there a difference between discipline and abuse?**

THE UN CONVENTION ON THE RIGHTS OF THE CHILD

The Convention gives children and young people over 40 rights. These include the right to:

- Special protection and assistance.
- Access to education and health care.
- The right to develop their personalities, abilities and talents to the fullest potential.
- Grow up in an environment of love, happiness and understanding.
- Be informed about their rights and how to achieve them.

All of the rights in the Convention apply to all children and young people without discrimination.

PROTECTING THE RIGHTS OF ELDERLY PEOPLE

In many parts of the world, elderly people are treated with respect and receive the care they deserve. Sadly, in our society elderly people are sometimes denied their basic rights. The term 'elder abuse' is used to describe cruel or degrading treatment of elderly people. The charity Action on Elder Abuse (AEA) works in the UK and Ireland to protect older adults. There is concern that elderly people in nursing homes are being denied their basic human rights and dignity, but sometimes this abuse takes place at home. For example:

- **Physical abuse:** Some elderly people can easily be assaulted by a stronger person and receive rough treatment. Assault also includes forcing a person to take medication that they do not need, perhaps to sedate them.

- **Psychological abuse:** An elderly person might be threatened to make them follow the wishes of others; for example, being told that their grandchildren might not be brought to visit them.

- **Neglect:** Some elderly people need assistance to provide for their basic needs and rely on the help of others. There is growing concern that some elderly people in care homes are suffering from neglect.

RESEARCH ACTIVITY

In February 2010, **The Northern Ireland Human Rights Commission** launched an investigation into the human rights of older people in care. It is focusing on the 256 nursing homes in Northern Ireland.

Use the Internet to research the following:
- What human rights might an elderly person in a nursing home be denied?

- Find out more about the investigation. You could use the following link: http://www.nihrc.org/index.php?option=com_content&task=view&id=96&Itemid=105

SHOULD HUMAN RIGHTS EVER BE LIMITED?

Sometimes when a person claims a right, this can cause another person's right to be violated. This is why rights have to be carefully balanced against each other. Here are some issues to consider:

- **Does everyone have the right to freedom of speech?** Everyone is entitled to his or her own opinion. However, there is debate about whether freedom of speech should be limited in some cases. A person may have extreme racist views. Is it right for these views to be printed in a newspaper or heard on the radio as they could lead to hate crime? This would mean that another person's right to live in safety was being denied. It is necessary to balance which right is the most important.

- **Do criminals have rights?** A person who commits a crime and receives a prison sentence has their right to freedom limited. This is partly to keep society safe from the person who has committed an anti-social act and partly to serve as a punishment. There is divided opinion as to whether a criminal in prison should have other rights denied as well. A prisoner is still a human being and has to be treated with basic human dignity. However, some people feel very angry when they hear that prisoners have more material goods than many people who are not in prison! A difficult question is whether prisoners should lose other rights as well as their right to freedom.

• **Is privacy more important than security?** Most people would agree that national security and crime prevention are important issues. However, there is growing concern that the price to be paid for this is an invasion of privacy. Since the year 2000, government authorities, such as the police, Customs and secret services, have had the right to monitor email messages and demand information about phone calls. Security forces say they have the right to collect information that may help to prevent serious crime, such as terrorist activity. Some people feel these laws deny the right to privacy and are open to abuse. There is an increasing amount of personal information stored in electronic databases and some people are worried about who might have access to these details. There are different opinions about the use of security cameras. They can deter crime and help identify offenders, but some people resent being 'spied on' whether they are in a shop, a doctor's waiting room or just walking in the street.

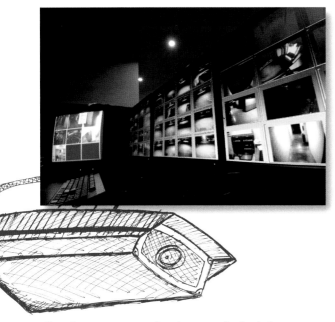

• **Why do some people give up their rights voluntarily?** Some people decide to give up their rights voluntarily. This may be because they regard something else as being more important, for example, their culture or religion. A Muslim fasting during the month of Ramadan will give up food and drink during the hours of daylight, while some people feel that they should avoid alcohol as a lifestyle choice. Contestants on TV reality shows, such as 'Big Brother' have voluntarily given up their right to privacy, in the hope of fame and fortune. Most people would not have a problem with those who choose to give up their rights voluntarily.

DISCUSSION

Look at the Universal Declaration of Human Rights on page 46.

Which rights from the Declaration might be denied if people do not have freedom of speech?

On the other hand, which rights could be denied if everyone is allowed to express their views publicly?

ACTIVITY

Read the case study that follows.

• Assess which rights are being infringed or ignored.

• Do you think this denial of rights can be justified?

CASE STUDY: GUANTANAMO BAY

There is a US Naval base in Guantanamo Bay in Cuba. A detention centre there has been the cause of controversy since it opened in 2002. Following the threat of terrorist attacks, particularly by extremist groups such as al-Qaeda, the Guantanamo Bay centre has been used to detain those suspected of terrorism. There have been serious concerns about the treatment of prisoners, many of whom have not been charged with any specific offence. By 2005 an estimated 600 prisoners had been detained without trial. Pictures were shown in the media of prisoners with hoods over their faces and wearing shackles on wrists and ankles. Newspaper reports made allegations of prisoners being tortured, beaten, deprived of sleep and exposed to extremes of temperature.

Human rights organisations have campaigned for many years to have the detention centre closed. Under international human rights law, everyone has the right to a fair trial and cannot be detained for long periods of time without charge. Torture and other forms of ill treatment, whether to punish, intimidate or obtain a confession, are a denial of a prisoner's basic human rights.

Others have justified the harsh treatment of these prisoners. In the war against terrorism, it is argued that such measures are undesirable but necessary.

If a prisoner is thought to be connected to a terrorist attack, should they be denied their human rights?

In January 2009, President Obama announced that the Guantanamo Bay detention centre would be closed within a year. Two years on, at the time of writing, the White House has admitted that it will be a while yet before the centre closes. There are currently 174 inmates in the prison and it now seems likely that nearly 50 of them could be detained indefinitely.

RIGHTS AND RESPONSIBILITIES: GETTING THE BALANCE CORRECT

It is important for people to know their rights. This is to ensure that they are not denied basic freedoms and standards of living and that they know they will be treated fairly in society. Human Rights are unconditional and for everyone. However, it is also important that people are aware of their responsibilities as well. Rights and responsibilities go together and there needs to be the correct balance between the two.

Sometimes people seem more concerned with their rights than their responsibilities. The problem with this attitude is that it can lead to people becoming very selfish and not thinking about the rights of others. If you ever think "It's my right to …" then try to think of a responsibility you have as well!

Here are some of the responsibilities a person has in their community:

• **Taking responsibility for children:** Parenthood brings a number of responsibilities. Children have the right to be provided for, protected from harm and educated. Parents and carers have the responsibility to ensure that these needs are met, by providing food, clothing, shelter, love and discipline. Parents should not neglect their children or fail to take proper responsibility for them.

• **Law and order:** It is the duty of every citizen to obey the law of the land, as laws have been passed by a democratically elected government and are there to protect everybody's interests. It is also the duty of every responsible person to report a crime and give the police full co-operation.

• **Paying taxes:** Taxes and rates are paid for the benefit of the whole community, whether to fund the NHS, the local library or the council's recycling scheme. It is irresponsible, and illegal, to try to avoid these payments.

• **Participating in a democratic society:** Voting in a democracy is an important right, yet it is denied to many people in the world today. Therefore, people who do have this right should act responsibly and use it.

• **Living a 'greener' lifestyle:** Showing responsibility towards the environment is becoming increasingly important. This can involve recycling as much as possible, considering renewable sources of energy for the home and not owning a bigger car than is needed.

Draw two spider diagrams like the ones below.

· Think of as many examples as you can for your **rights** and **responsibilities** at school.

· Now write down how the two are connected. For example: "I have the right to be educated and I have the responsibility to meet homework deadlines."

evaluation

Evaluate how the Universal Declaration of Human Rights can help people who are suffering from injustice.

EXAM FOCUS

This section will appear at the end of every chapter. It will help you to develop your exam skills.

Different styles of exam question on your paper will test different skills. One of these is to **show that you can apply your knowledge and understanding**.

The following question tests this skill:

(a) Name **one** way a person can play an active part in their local community.

[1 mark]

(b) Explain **one** reason why people should try to take an active role in their local community. [2 marks]

(c) Explain **one** way in which pressure groups can bring about a change in society.

[2 marks]

Question taken from CCEA's GCSE Learning for Life and Work Modular Specimen Assessment Materials, Unit 3: Local and Global Citizenship Specimen Paper (2009)

To gain full marks for (b) and (c) you must write a detailed explanation, for example:

"A pressure group might ask a celebrity to get involved. This could raise the profile of their campaign and influence the government to change their policies. It will also increase the public's interest in the campaign."

Chapter three

THE ROLE OF SOCIETY AND GOVERNMENT IN SAFEGUARDING HUMAN RIGHTS

CHAPTER SUMMARY

In this chapter you will be studying:

- The law relating to equal opportunities and discrimination.
- Why some groups of people become marginalised in society today.
- The responsibility of the government in protecting people's rights.

INTRODUCTION

FAIR TREATMENT
EQUAL TREATMENT

FAIR TREATMENT AND EQUAL TREATMENT

Here is a key question to consider:
Is treating someone fairly the same as treating them equally?

Consider a doctor's waiting room. There is a man with a sports injury, a small child with an upset stomach and an elderly lady who needs a flu injection. They all expect the doctor to treat them fairly. However, what would their reaction be if the doctor decided to treat them equally and gave everyone the flu injection? Would this be treating everyone fairly? Of course not!

Fair treatment and equal treatment are not necessarily the same thing.

Treating people fairly means considering their individual needs and acting accordingly. Often, fairness means taking differences into account, but in some cases fairness means ignoring difference and treating people equally. Think about your school. Pupils can choose some of their GCSE subjects based on what they enjoy and are good at. It would be unfair to expect everyone to study the same subjects in the same way. On the other hand, everyone has the right not to be bullied at school, so it is fair that an anti-bullying policy will apply to everyone equally.

Attempting to get the balance right between what is fair and what is equal can be difficult, particularly when people have different needs and expectations.

EQUAL OPPORTUNITIES AND THE LAW

WHAT IS MEANT BY EQUAL OPPORTUNITY?

This term is often used when talking about employment, but it can also refer to other areas, such as education. 'Equal opportunity' means that everyone has the same chance as everyone else to receive an education or promotion at work. For example, a person should never be treated unfairly because of factors such as gender, age, race, religion or disability.

In the world of work, or in education, if a person needs to be selected, then they should be judged by their skills, experience and personal qualities. When staff are being recruited or considered for promotion, equal treatment is necessary to make sure that there are equal opportunities for everyone.

Some people say that this is not enough and that equal outcomes must also be considered. This means ensuring that minority groups are represented equally on the workforce, perhaps by encouraging applications from people with a particular background. However, '**positive discrimination**' – giving someone a job just because they are a member of a minority group – is illegal.

Equal opportunity is also important within the context of health care and social services. The same opportunity to receive treatment, care and other services should be provided to everyone. The different aspects of each person – gender, age, ethnic origin, for example – also need to be considered, remembering that fair treatment does not always mean treating everyone in the same way.

All citizens have the right to equal opportunity whether they have only lived here a short time, or if their family has been here for generations. There are laws in place that make discrimination illegal and there are government agencies working to ensure the fair treatment of all people.

THE NORTHERN IRELAND ACT 1998

The Northern Ireland Act is a lengthy and detailed Act of Parliament, covering the arrangements for the devolved rule of Northern Ireland. It is divided into 101 sections, and it is **Section 75** which deals with equal opportunities and the need to promote good community relations.

Section 75 of the Northern Ireland Act came into force on 1st January 2000 and it placed a legal obligation on public authorities to promote equality of opportunity:

- between persons of different religious belief, political opinion, racial group, age, marital status or sexual orientation.

- between men and women generally.

- between persons with a disability and persons without.

- between persons with dependants and persons without.

Wordbox

Legal Obligation
An action which must be carried out or a service that must be provided, as there is a law in place to make sure this happens.

Wordbox

Public Authority
This is a group or organisation, such as a local council or Education and Library Board, which has been given official power to govern or administrate in the local community. This responsibility is usually given by the government.

In addition, public authorities are also required to promote good relations between people of different religious belief, political opinion and racial group. Public authorities include groups such as the Northern Ireland Housing Executive, Education and Library boards, local councils, the National Health Service and the Northern Ireland Civil Service.

In Northern Ireland, the Office of the First Minister and deputy First Minister has the responsibility for making sure that this act is carried out. The OFMDFM was created under the Northern Ireland Act and is answerable to the Northern Ireland Assembly.

ACTIVITY

Use bullet points to make your own list of the groups of people whose rights are protected under Section 75 of the Northern Ireland Act. How many different groups of people does this legislation protect?

DISCUSSION

Do you think this list covers everyone who might face discrimination in society?

Can you think of any examples of people/ groups that are not covered?

Wordbox

Legislation
This term refers to laws which have been made by the government.

DISCRIMINATION

Many people in society today face discrimination and this negative treatment can take different forms. Sometimes a person, or group of people, is made to feel that they are excluded from society and cannot play a full role. The term '**marginalised**' is often used for people who are treated in this way. Discrimination can also be more direct and involve the use of violent or abusive behaviour, for example assault, threatening behaviour, damage to property, graffiti, name-calling and verbal insults.

There is a need for laws to ensure the fair and equal treatment of all citizens. It is against the law for a person to be discriminated against because of factors such as age, race, religion, gender, or disability, for example. The law recognises that discrimination is not simply unfairness. To be discriminated against means to be treated in a less favourable way than other people. This includes the workplace, at school or having access to important services, such as healthcare.

The laws that seek to protect potentially vulnerable groups of people often refer to four types of discrimination:

1. **Direct** – A person is treated less favourably because of age, race, religion, gender, etc.

2. **Indirect** – An unfair condition is made, deliberately designed to exclude certain people.

3. **Victimisation** – This means to single someone out for less favourable treatment, perhaps because they have complained about discrimination in the past.

4. **Harassment** – This includes name-calling and spiteful remarks and creating an intimidating or hostile environment for another person.

If a person is treated in any of these ways at work or in the community, then they may be facing discrimination and there are laws in place to protect them.

THE LAW IN NORTHERN IRELAND

Is discrimination a cause for concern in Northern Ireland? Using the groups given in Section 75, here are some examples of ways in which people have their rights protected. Other laws promoting equal opportunity are also considered. However, perhaps the hardest challenge to tackle is trying to change the prejudiced attitudes of a small minority of people.

Religious belief

Since the 1970s, the government has been taking action against religious discrimination in the workplace. It was recognised by many people that Roman Catholics were underrepresented in senior and management posts and were also more likely to be unemployed than Protestants. The Fair Employment Act 1976 prohibited discrimination in the workplace because of a person's religion. In 1989 a legal duty was placed on employers to monitor the religious background of their employees.

The Fair Employment and Treatment (Northern Ireland) Order 1998 (FETO) made it unlawful to discriminate against someone because of religious belief or political opinion. This legislation is concerned with equality of opportunity for both the Protestant and Catholic communities.

Northern Ireland has traditionally been seen as a predominantly Christian community. Although people who follow other religious traditions have lived here for centuries, they have always been in a very small minority. Now the situation is changing and Hindus, Muslims, Bahá'ís and Sikhs, for example, form an increasingly significant section of the population. People from non-Christian backgrounds must also be given equality of opportunity in schools, the workplace and society, as well as people who have no religious faith at all.

Political opinion

Traditionally, political opinion and religious belief in Northern Ireland have been closely linked, with most Protestants voting for Unionist parties and most Catholics voting for Nationalist parties.

Discrimination due to political opinion is illegal and is covered by the following legislation:

- The Fair Employment and Treatment (Northern Ireland) Order 1998 (FETO).
- Section 75 of the Northern Ireland Act 1998.
- Human Rights Act 1998.

Section 75 places an obligation on public authorities to promote good relationships between people of different religious belief, political opinion and racial group.

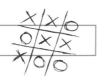

A CONTROVERSIAL ISSUE …

Should religious or political symbols be banned in public places?

Some people believe that they should, in the interest of promoting good relationships between people of different religious or political beliefs. On the other hand, is it religious discrimination to be told that you are not allowed to wear a piece of clothing or jewellery?

Consider the following examples:

· A town hall displays the Union Jack for the 12th of July.

· A Muslim girl is told she cannot wear a hijab (headscarf) in school.

· Workers in a government building are told they cannot wear poppies for Remembrance Day.

· A Sikh man in a UK prison is not allowed to wear a turban.

· A nurse is not allowed to wear a Christian cross on a neck chain.

For each example, discuss the following questions:

· What are the different points of view involved in the controversy?

· Has discrimination been shown in the example, and if so, in what way?

· Do you agree or disagree with the decision made in each situation?

Racial group

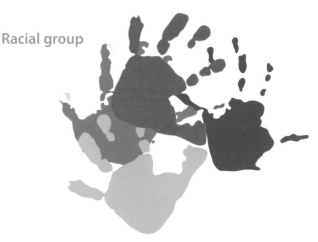

People from a variety of different ethnic backgrounds are choosing to live in Northern Ireland. This means that racial diversity needs to be respected and understood, and any inequalities arising from a person's ethnic origin need to be tackled.

The Race Relations Order came into effect in 1997. It outlaws discrimination on the grounds of colour, race, nationality, ethnicity or national origin. The RRO makes it unlawful to discriminate in employment, education, and in the provision of goods and services. You cannot be refused a hotel room or a table in a restaurant, for example, because of ethnic origins.

The Traveller community is specifically identified in the RRO as a group which is protected against racial discrimination. This means that Irish Travellers are included in the 'racial group' category of Section 75 of the Northern Ireland Act 1998.

THE IRISH TRAVELLER COMMUNITY – THE FACTS

Although travellers are protected by law from discrimination, they are one of the most marginalised groups in society. Travellers are disadvantaged in almost every area of life, suffering from unemployment, poverty and poor health.

· 92% of Travellers have no GCSEs or higher.

· Only 10% of Travellers are over 40 years of age and only 1% are over 65 years.

· Only 35% of Travellers aged 16-74 are employed or have the means to support themselves financially.

Statistics taken from http://www.equalityni.org

Age

The Northern Ireland Act places an obligation on all public authorities to promote equality of opportunity regardless of age. This means that no one should face discrimination because they are considered to be either too young or too old.

Old
Young

DISCUSSION

Read the Case Studies that follow. They are both examples of age discrimination.

Is the discrimination direct or indirect? (see pages 60– 61)

CASE STUDY: JOAN

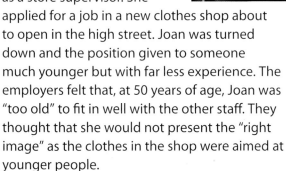

Joan has considerable experience in the retail trade as a store supervisor. She applied for a job in a new clothes shop about to open in the high street. Joan was turned down and the position given to someone much younger but with far less experience. The employers felt that, at 50 years of age, Joan was "too old" to fit in well with the other staff. They thought that she would not present the "right image" as the clothes in the shop were aimed at younger people.

CASE STUDY: ROBERT

Robert has a part-time job in a local garage, working in the evening or at weekends as he is still at school. Although the shifts are supposed to vary, Robert always seems to end up working on Saturday evening – the shift no one wants to do. He was told it was because he was never there when the rota was planned. Robert thinks this is unfair as the rota is always planned during the daytime when he is at school.

The Employment Equality (Age) Regulations (Northern Ireland) 2006 specifically deals with discrimination in the workplace or in education.

A person does not have full adult rights until they reach 18 years of age. However, younger people should still be treated with dignity and respect; they are entitled to their own opinion and have the right to be taken seriously. Young people have the right to information to help them make informed choices about important issues, such as health and careers. However, young people do not have the same rights to goods and services as an adult. This is because some things are age-restricted, such as buying alcoholic drink or watching an 18 rated film.

Older people also have the right to be treated with dignity and respect, even if they are not as active or independent as they once were. The majority of older people want to make their own decisions and contribute fully in society; they want to feel valued and carry on doing the things they enjoy. Sadly, some older people are marginalised by society, perhaps rarely leaving their home and suffering from low self-esteem.

Old School is Cool

Age Is Wisdom

Fight Ageism

Age Rage

Respect Our Rights

Gender

Section 75 of the Northern Ireland Act seeks to promote equality between men and women generally. **Sexual discrimination** means less favourable treatment on the grounds of a person's gender. (It does not include sexual orientation, which is dealt with separately.)

The Sex Discrimination (Northern Ireland) Order has been in force since 1976. In all areas of life – for example, work, education, and healthcare – it is unlawful to discriminate because of a person's sex or whether or not they are married. A woman should not be at a disadvantage because she is pregnant and will need to take time off on maternity leave; her job should be kept for her to come back to. This is an example of treating people differently in order to be fair. Special allowances need to be made during pregnancy. If a woman has to be absent from work for hospital appointments or take time off on sick leave, this should not count against her if a future promotion is ever being considered.

There are some exceptions to the Sex Discrimination Order, where a job specifically requires either a man or a woman. An acting job might need a woman, while the vacancy for a prison officer in a men's prison could be made available to male applicants only.

Sexual harassment is also unlawful under the Sex Discrimination Order. This includes:

- Physical contact (such as unnecessary touching).
- Verbal contact (such as sexual remarks).
- Non-verbal contact (such as sexual gestures).

Marital status

Section 75 of the Northern Ireland Act promotes equality of opportunity for everyone, regardless of whether they are married, single, widowed, divorced, separated or living together. A person should not be treated differently to another person because they are married. For example, it cannot be assumed that an applicant for a job is more likely to be settled and responsible than an unmarried person. Some people may hold strong personal views about marriage, divorce or living together, but these opinions should not influence how another person is treated.

Having dependants

Equal opportunities should be available for all people, whether or not they have dependants to care for. Having a dependant usually means being responsible for the care of:

- A child.
- An elderly person.
- Someone who has a chronic illness or disability.

More women than men are in the role of primary carer for a dependant person, and would be more likely to face discrimination in employment because of this. Some children have to care for a parent who is disabled or who has an addiction problem. There is concern that child carers should not be at a disadvantage with their education.

Sexual Orientation

The Northern Ireland Act supports equality of opportunity regardless of a person's sexual orientation. The most recent law that has been passed is The Equality Act (Sexual Orientation) Regulations (NI) 2006. It is unlawful to discriminate against a person because of their sexual orientation, or what you think their sexual orientation might be. This law applies to schools, higher education, the workplace and society as a whole.

Many people in society today are unwilling to accept people who are homosexual as neighbours, friends or work colleagues. There is still a problem today with people being marginalised because of their sexuality and being the victim of hate crime.

DISCUSSION

Read the following examples.

What type of discrimination has taken place in each?

Which do you think is the most serious?

What law has been broken in each scenario?

- In an interview for a promotion at work, Joanna is asked about her family arrangements. Her boss then assumes she would not be able to do the job properly as she has too many commitments at home.

- A young Asian couple enquire about a flat for rent. They are told the flat has already been let. The landlord thinks some of the other tenants in the building would object to neighbours from an ethnic minority group.

- A transport company needs to hire a lorry driver. They do not think a woman would fit in very well as all the other drivers are men. The job advertisement says that applicants must be over 5 foot 10 inches tall.

- Sylvia uses a wheelchair. She and her partner go out to a busy restaurant without a reservation. There is one table available, but they are told the restaurant is fully booked, as there is concern that Sylvia's wheelchair will get in the way.

- There is a lot of gossip in the office about whether the new clerical assistant is homosexual. He has been the victim of bad jokes and spiteful comments. Some of the men in the office are trying to avoid contact with him.

Disability

Having a disability could mean a problem with communication, sight or mobility. It may also include a mental health or learning difficulty. A person with a disability has the same right to equality of opportunity as everyone else. As well as being one of the groups in Section 75, people with disabilities have their rights protected by law in the Disability Discrimination Act of 1995 and the Human Rights Act 1998.

People with a disability often face many problems, such as lower levels of income and difficulties accessing public buildings and transport. Some disabled people feel marginalised and excluded from society. However, with improved technology and change in public attitudes, a greater number of disabled people can enjoy independent living and follow the career of their choice.

DISABILITY – SOME FACTS AND FIGURES

- There are approximately 201,000 disabled adults in Northern Ireland.

- 83,000 are men and 118,000 are women.

- 154,800 are of working age.

- 14,600 are disabled children.

- It is often physical and attitudinal barriers which disadvantage the person more than their physical or mental impairment.

- People with a disability are more than twice as likely to have no formal qualifications as people without disabilities.

Statistics taken from: http://www.workingwithdiversity.org

CONSEQUENCES OF DISCRIMINATION

PEOPLE MARGINALISED BY SOCIETY

The different groups already mentioned are protected from discrimination by law. There are other groups of people, not protected by law, who may find themselves pushed to the margins of society. They include:

- people who are suffering from a long-term illness or mental health issues.

- those who are homeless.

- young people leaving care.

- ex-offenders.

- people who are unemployed, particularly those with few qualifications and skills.

All people need to feel valued by the community in which they live and to know that they can play a full role in society. A person who is marginalised in society can suffer from loneliness and feelings of low self confidence and self-esteem. It is also important for the peace and security of everyone in the community that no groups of people are marginalised. A society is a group of people living and working together. If some individuals, or groups of people, feel that they have been deliberately excluded then the society is not working as it should.

The following verse was written by a German anti-Nazi activist.

Why should standing up for all people in the community be the concern of everyone?

"First they came for the Jews
and I did not speak out – because I was not a Jew.

Then they came for the communists
and I did not speak out – because I was not a communist.

Then they came for the trade unionists
and I did not speak out – because I was not a trade unionist.

Then they came for me –
and by then there was no one left to speak out for me."

Pastor Martin Niemöller

HATE CRIME IN NORTHERN IRELAND

Newspaper headlines suggest that even though efforts are being made to protect the rights of everyone in society and promote equality of opportunity, hate crime is a serious problem. The vast majority of people here have positive attitudes towards their neighbours. However, there is a small minority who target sections of the community for abuse and attack.

A hate crime is a criminal offence mainly motivated by the victim being different to the attacker. This difference could be because of race, ethnicity or sexual orientation – or any other reason that makes the attacker feel justified in inflicting physical or mental suffering on their victim.

Hate crime is not something new in Northern Ireland. The sectarian violence of 'the troubles' at the end of the last century was an example of hate crime, though the term was not used at the time. People were killed, intimidated or subjected to violence because they were seen as being 'different', and therefore a target for attack. When violence began in the early 1970s, whole areas became exclusively Protestant or Catholic as people from the other 'group' were intimidated out of their homes. Now, it is people from ethnic minorities who are facing threats of violence to themselves or their property and having to leave their homes in fear.

Not all incidents of hate crime are reported to the police. This may be for the following reasons:

- Victims may not want to be seen complaining about their neighbours.

- There may be difficulties with language.

- They may feel that there is little that can be done about it.

- They may be too afraid to speak out.

- There may be a lack of knowledge about laws regarding racial crime.

- They may fear the attacks will get worse.

NEWS ITEM

RACISM IN NORTHERN IRELAND

More than 100 Romanian people have fled their homes in Belfast, saying they feel intimidated after a series of attacks. BBC News examines the problem of racism in Northern Ireland.

When the police in Northern Ireland started recording racially motivated crime in 1996 there were just 41 incidents.

Last year there were nearly 1,000.

In part the increase in the number of incidents can be explained by the increase in the ethnic minority population.

There was a growth in the number of migrants coming to Northern Ireland following the paramilitary ceasefires and the accession of central and eastern European countries to the European Union.

Northern Ireland's established Chinese, Indian and Vietnamese communities were joined by thousands more ethnic minorities from across the world.

However there is also the suggestion that a legacy of Northern Ireland's sectarian conflict is a "culture of intolerance" that leads to violence against people not just of a different religion but also those of a different ethnic background.

Source: BBC NEWS, 17 June 2009,
http://news.bbc.co.uk/go/pr/fr/-/1/hi/northern_ireland/8104978.stm

Wordbox

Accession
This term can be used when a newcomer becomes a member of an established group, for example, when a country joins the European Economic Union it is said to have accession to the EEC.

ACTIVITY

Reports of race hate crime in Northern Ireland, like the one in the news item opposite, have been appearing in the media for the last 5 years or so. This has led to some people describing Northern Ireland as *"The race hate capital of Europe"*.

- Do you agree that this is a fair description?

- Write a letter to the editor of a newspaper giving your view on this comment about Northern Ireland.

Sexual orientation and hate crime

Some people experience hate crime because of their sexual orientation. **The Rainbow Project** is a voluntary organisation providing advice and support for homosexual men. In June 2009 The Rainbow Project published a report on homophobic hate crime in Northern Ireland called 'Through our eyes'. Their research was based on interviews with over 1,000 people. Here are some of their findings:

The extent of hate crime

- 39% of the people surveyed had been the victim of a crime in the last 3 years.

- 52% believed the crime was motivated by homophobia.

The nature of the crimes

- 66% had suffered verbal insults, intimidation and harassment.

- 29% had been physically assaulted.

- 30% had been threatened with violence.

Who commits hate crime?

- 93% of attacks were carried out by 'white' people; only a very small minority of attacks were carried out by members of an ethnic minority group.

Reporting hate crime

- 64% of homophobic incidents go unreported, often because the victims did not think the attack would be taken seriously.

For more information visit:
http://www.rainbow-project.org/assets/publications/through_our_eyes.pdf

DISCUSSION

What action could be taken by each of the following to make sure that all hate crime becomes a thing of the past?

- Individuals
- Schools
- The police
- The government

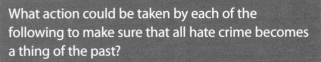

THE OFFICE OF THE FIRST MINISTER AND DEPUTY FIRST MINISTER

The Northern Ireland Act 1998 led to the formation of the Northern Ireland Assembly. The First Minister is a member of the largest party in the Assembly and the deputy First Minister is a member of the second largest. Usually one would represent a Unionist party and the other would be a Nationalist. Together they run the Office of the First Minister and deputy First Minister (OFMDFM) and share responsibilities with each other. This office has a number of important duties, such as economic policy and improving public services. It also has the responsibility to promote equality of opportunity and good relations, and tackle poverty and social exclusion.

Two Junior Ministers assist the First Minister and deputy First Minister in carrying out the work of the OFMDFM.

At the time of writing, Peter Robinson of the Democratic Unionist Party is First Minister and Martin McGuinness of Sinn Féin is deputy First Minister.

Wordbox

Economic policy
This term refers to the action that a government might take in order to manage the country's money efficiently. This can involve setting interest rates and deciding on the government budget. The aim is for businesses to make a profit and for people's living standards to get better.

Public Services
This term refers to the services provided by the government to its citizens, such as education, healthcare, repairs to roads and collection of household waste.

Equality issues are dealt with by the Equality Directorate of the OFMDFM and the work of this department is co-ordinated by a Director of Equality.

There are two divisions within the Equality Directorate:

- Equality, Rights and Social Need Division.
- Good Relations and Reconciliation Division.

EQUALITY, RIGHTS AND SOCIAL NEED DIVISION

This Division is made up of the following departments:

1. Anti-Poverty Unit
   This unit has overall responsibility for tackling poverty and social exclusion. It aims to help vulnerable groups of people have better access to education, housing, health and employment.

2. Equality and Human Rights Unit
   This unit has the responsibility for promoting the

legal obligations in Section 75 of the Northern Ireland Act 1998. The Equality and Human Rights Unit works closely with the Equality Commission to make sure that people are aware of the support available to them. Employers also need to understand their duties and responsibilities towards employees.

3. Gender and Sexual Orientation Equality Unit

The GSOEU develops and co-ordinates policies across the Northern Ireland Civil Service. Their aim is to promote equality and tackle any cases of discrimination due to gender or sexual orientation.

4. Equality Legislation

This unit is responsible for developing anti-discrimination laws so that people can have their rights protected across a range of public services.

5. Equality Research

Research is carried out so that statistics are available for other units, to help them meet needs and work effectively. This unit is closely linked to the Good Relations Research carried out for the Good Relations and Reconciliation Division below and their work may overlap.

GOOD RELATIONS AND RECONCILIATION DIVISION

This Division is also made up of five departments:

1. Community Relations Unit

This unit was established in 1987. It aims to heal divisions in society by increasing cross-community contact and co-operation. The Community Relations Unit also works to encourage mutual respect and an appreciation of cultural diversity.

2. Race Equality Unit

This unit aims to promote racial equality in Northern Ireland. It is responsible for making policies to ensure that people from ethnic minority groups are treated fairly. This is the vision of the unit:

> *"A society in which racial diversity is supported, understood, valued and respected, where racism in any of its forms is not tolerated and where we can all live together as a society and enjoy equality of opportunity and equal protection."*
>
> Source: http://www.ofmdfmni.gov.uk

3. Victims Unit

This unit is concerned with people who are victims of 'the troubles' in Northern Ireland. It aims to raise awareness of the issues affecting these people and to co-ordinate activities to support them.

4. Children and Young Peoples' Unit

This unit was established to make sure that the rights and needs of children and young people are given high priority. Some of the most important concerns include health, education, safety, economic well-being and respect for children's rights.

TIMELINE: ANTI-DISCRIMINATION LAW IN NORTHERN IRELAND

1970	1976	1997	1999	2000
Equal pay for men and women becomes law; a woman can no longer be paid less than a man if she is doing the same job.	Sex Discrimination Law is introduced; a person can not be treated less favourably because of gender or marital status. Fair Employment Legislation makes it unlawful to treat people differently because of religious belief or political opinion.	Race Relations Law is introduced; it is illegal to discriminate because of colour, race, nationality, ethnicity or national origin. The Traveller community is specifically identified as a racial group which is protected against discrimination.	The Equality Commission is established to promote equality of opportunity and good relationships in society.	The Equality Commission has new responsibilities in relation to disability discrimination. A duty has now been placed on all employers and service providers to make sure that people with a disability can have access to their premises.

5. Good Relations Research

Research is carried out so that statistics are available to support the work of the other units.

THE EQUALITY COMMISSION FOR NORTHERN IRELAND

The Equality Commission is a governmental organisation working to safeguard individual and group rights. It also seeks to promote equality in society and the workplace. The following information is taken from their website (www.equalityni.org):

"The Equality Commission for Northern Ireland is an independent public body established under the Northern Ireland Act 1998.

Our vision: The Equality Commission has the vision of Northern Ireland as a shared, integrated and inclusive place, a society where difference is respected and valued, based on equality and fairness for the entire community.

Our mission: To advance equality, promote equality of opportunity, encourage good relations and challenge discrimination through promotion, advice and enforcement.

The Commission's duties and functions are set out in the legislation for which we have responsibility. General duties include:

- working towards the elimination of discrimination.
- promoting equality of opportunity and encouraging good practice.
- promoting affirmative/positive action.
- promoting good relations between people of different racial groups.
- overseeing the implementation and effectiveness of the statutory duty on public authorities to promote equality and good relations.

- overseeing the disability duties on public authorities.
- monitoring, jointly with the NI Human Rights Commission, the implementation of the UN Convention on the Rights of Persons with Disabilities.
- keeping the relevant legislation under review."

For further information visit: www.equalityni.org

CHECK YOUR LEARNING

Explain how each of the following promotes equality and tackles discrimination. Write a short paragraph for each one.

1. The Office of the First Minister and deputy First Minister.
2. The Equality Commission for Northern Ireland.
3. Section 75 of the Northern Ireland Act.

evaluation

Evaluate the effectiveness of government organisations in protecting human rights.

DISCUSSION

- From the timeline below, which three developments do you think have been the most significant in the history of anti-discrimination law?

- Justify your choice to the person beside you.

2003	2005	2006	2007	2008
It is now illegal to discriminate in the workplace because of a person's sexual orientation.	The Disability Discrimination Act is now extended to schools through the Special Educational Needs and Disability Order (SENDO).	It is now illegal to treat someone less favourably because of their age as the Employment Equality (Age) Regulations (Northern Ireland) 2006 come into force.	People who are diagnosed with cancer, MS, HIV and mental ill-health are now protected from disability discrimination.	Employers must protect employees from sexual harassment by customers or clients as well as from other workers – Sex Discrimination (Amendment) Regulations (NI) 2008.

Rewarding Learning

EXAM FOCUS

This section will appear at the end of every chapter. It will help you to develop your exam skills.

In chapters 1 and 2, we looked at the skills of **demonstrating your knowledge and understanding** and **applying your knowledge and understanding.**

The following question will give you practice at both these skills:

(a) Name a Northern Ireland organisation that has responsibility for safeguarding Human Rights.   [1 mark]

(b) Explain **one** way the First and deputy First Minister can promote and protect Human Rights.   [2 marks]

(c) Identify and explain **one** equal opportunities law. [2 marks]

Question taken from CCEA's GCSE Learning for Life and Work Modular Paper, Unit 3: Local and Global Citizenship Summer 2010, GLW41.

When answering parts (b) and (c) identify your example clearly, then develop your explanation.

You could answer part (b) in the following way:

"The Equality and Human Rights Unit are part of the OFMDFM. They can appoint a committee to investigate Human Rights in Northern Ireland. They also promote equality and make sure people know what laws are there to protect them."

Continue this answer by answering part (c).

INFORMATION F

The total mark for th
Quality of written co
Figures in brackets pr
question or part questi

Chapter four

NON-GOVERNMENTAL ORGANISATIONS (NGOs)

CHAPTER SUMMARY

In this chapter you will be studying:

- **What is meant by social equality and social justice.**
- **The causes and consequences of inequality and injustice.**
- **How NGOs tackle these issues at home and in the wider world.**

* Remember CCEA reviews the NGOs every three years, so ensure you check the CCEA website for an up-to-date list.

INTRODUCTION

IT'S AN UNFAIR WORLD!

The world we live in is not fair. Some people have wealth most of us can only dream of, while others face such appalling poverty that it can be difficult for us to even image their daily struggle for survival.

Look at the panel *'If the world were a village of 100 people'*:

What statements suggest that many people in the world do not receive fair or equal treatment?

IF THE WORLD WERE A VILLAGE OF 100 PEOPLE

If we could reduce the world's population to a village of precisely 100 people, with all existing human ratios remaining the same, the demographics would look something like this: The village would have 60 Asians, 14 Africans, 12 Europeans, 8 Latin Americans, 5 from the USA and Canada, and 1 from the South Pacific.

---

51 would be male, 49 would be female

82 would be non-white; 18 white

67 would be non-Christian; 33 would be Christian

80 would live in substandard housing

67 would be unable to read

50 would be malnourished and 1 dying of starvation

33 would be without access to a safe water supply

39 would lack access to improved sanitation

24 would not have any electricity (and of the 76 that do have electricity, most would only use it for light at night.)

7 people would have access to the Internet

1 would have a college education

1 would have HIV

2 would be near birth; 1 near death

5 would control 32% of the entire world's wealth; all 5 would be US citizens

33 would be receiving – and attempting to live on – only 3% of the income of "the village"

Source: http://www.familycare.org/special-interest/if-the-world-were-a-village-of-100-people/

Some people talk about the world as being a **'global village.'** This means we are connected to every other citizen of the world. We are a community of people, regardless of different cultures and beliefs. Everyone should be concerned with issues of social equality and social justice, especially the people who are in a position to be able to do something positive.

Social equality means having equal rights under the law, such as the right to vote, own property and have freedom of speech. It also includes access to health care, education and other social services. Social inequality is often linked to economic inequality. If wealth is unevenly distributed, then people in poorer areas do not have the same access to good housing, healthcare and education that wealthier people do.

Social justice describes the movement towards a world which is fairer for all its citizens. It includes the idea that everyone is entitled to the same basic human rights, which should be available for everyone. People who are more financially secure can help towards this through taxation or voluntary contributions to NGOs. Some social injustice issues include unemployment, poverty and health.

SOCIAL INEQUALITY AND SOCIAL INJUSTICE

In Northern Ireland, as in the rest of the United Kingdom, most people have a good standard of living, although there are still exceptions to this. Many families live in run down or overcrowded housing. This can have a massive impact on children's lives, affecting their health, emotional well-being and achievement at school. Despite equal opportunity laws, some disabled people still face barriers to employment, while many elderly people have to survive on a low income.

However, the gap between rich and poor widens dramatically on a global scale. In many parts of the world, people die of starvation and lack basic amenities such as clean water. Healthcare and education might be barely adequate and not available to everyone on an equal basis. Some of these inequalities are the result of poverty or natural disasters. AIDS is also a serious concern, and again the world's most disadvantaged citizens are more likely to be at risk of contracting the disease.

The fact is that people who suffer from inequality are more likely to live in poverty with limited access to essential services such as healthcare and education.

Non-Governmental Organisations* play a vital role, by:

- Challenging social inequalities and injustice.
- Tackling the problems that they cause.

NGOs take action locally, nationally and globally. Fundraising and campaigns to raise awareness might take place in the local community. On a national level the work could include lobbying politicians or education programmes for schools. In a global context, NGOs can have an important role in supplying humanitarian aid.

* Note that some NGOs prefer to call themselves 'voluntary organisations' or 'charities'.

TEACHER'S NOTE
Any three of the following organisations are to be chosen for study.

NGO 1

THE NORTHERN IRELAND COUNCIL FOR VOLUNTARY ACTION

nicva
PROMOTING THE VOLUNTARY SECTOR

NICVA is a registered charity, but it is different to the other organisations covered in this chapter. NICVA does not work directly with people in need, but provides advice and support to those who do. NICVA can be described as an 'umbrella body' for the whole of the voluntary and community sector in Northern Ireland. The information it provides covers a wide range of issues, such as fundraising, research and how to lobby the government effectively.
Its website is: **www.nicva.org**

History

NICVA began its life in 1938 as the Northern Ireland Council for Social Services (NICSS) in response to high levels of unemployment in Northern Ireland. It championed a programme of social action through welfare clubs, youth hostel tours, YMCA summer camps and a Committee for Women.

In 1949 NICSS opened Pine Lodge, a home for the elderly on the Belmont Road, Belfast. This marked the Council's growing responsibility as an 'umbrella' organisation for projects which tackled social deprivation in the community.

Over the last 64 years NICSS has become increasingly well known. Its name changed to the Northern Ireland Council for Voluntary Action (NICVA) in 1986 in recognition of the expansion of the voluntary and community sector in Northern Ireland. Today NICVA represents the interests of its members and over 5,000 voluntary and community groups.

Vision, Mission and Values

NICVA has a vision of an effective voluntary and community sector which helps build a fair and equal society.

NICVA's mission is to represent and promote the voluntary and community sector in Northern Ireland by providing support and leadership to it.

NICVA's values include a commitment to justice and equality. They seek to oppose discrimination and promote diversity. NICVA is committed to positive social change to address issues such as poverty and exclusion. NICVA values people, whether staff or volunteers, and is also committed to pursuing a sustainable way of life.

How does NICVA achieve this?

Here are some examples of NICVA's key areas of work in providing advice and support to voluntary and community groups throughout Northern Ireland:

1. **Lobbying and campaigning** – Lobbying involves bringing an issue to the attention of a local councillor or MLA to encourage them to take action. Campaigning involves activities to raise awareness of important issues. These activities can be very important for voluntary organisations seeking to raise awareness for their work or an issue they are involved with. NICVA has developed a range of resources to help organisations do this effectively.

2. **Services** – NICVA offers a wide range of advice for organisations. This includes charity law, finance, human resources and many more.

3. **Charity advice** – NICVA's charity advice service offers information and practical help to charities about good governance. It is important for a charity to be an effective organisation, aware of the latest rules and regulations.

4. **Fundraising** – This is a vital area for most NGOs. NICVA has an experienced team available to help and advise organisations on all aspects of fundraising, from developing a policy on fundraising to practical ways to raise money.

5. **Research** – NICVA carry out research so information is available about what is going on in the voluntary and community sector. Their research covers four main areas: resources, people, performance and influence.

6. **Training** – NICVA organise various training courses throughout the year to make sure that people working in the voluntary sector have the skills they need. They also give specific training at the request of an organisation.

© Parkway Photography

7. **Human Resources** – It is important for any employer to be aware of employment law and to have good staff management. NICVA has a range of resources to help NGOs to stay well-informed about issues concerning employees.

8. **Information Technology** – NICVA offers support to NGOs to help them get the best out of their ICT. They also give advice about IT companies that offer discounts for charities and NGOs.

9. **Tax Effective Giving** – NICVA organises a scheme called Cheques for Charity. If a person who pays tax gives money to charity, then the amount of tax on the donation can be claimed back from the government. This is known as 'Gift Aid'. NICVA advises charities as to how this can benefit them and administers the scheme. It organises the tax refund which is credited to a donor's Cheques for Charity account, giving funds that can be used for further donations.

10. **Working with partners** – An essential part of NICVA's work is building partnerships with other organisations and representing the voluntary and community sector on various committees. Examples of NICVA'S partnerships include Stop Climate Chaos Northern Ireland, a coalition seeking to raise awareness of climate change, and the Women's Policy Forum, a group tackling women's issues.

NICVA's effectiveness

NICVA is a very successful and well-respected organisation in the voluntary and community sector in Northern Ireland. It is the specialist in all areas of practical organisation for charities, voluntary organisations and NGOs, and almost all groups in the voluntary sector use its training, advice and support services in some form. NICVA helps organisations to run more effectively, so they have more time and resources to spend on their particular area of work. It has also co-ordinated many successful lobbying campaigns and the tax-effective giving scheme it organises is now widely used when donating money to charity.

CHECK YOUR LEARNING

1. Explain briefly how and when NICVA started.

2. NICVA is an 'umbrella body'. What does this mean?

3. What are NICVA's vision, mission and values? Write a sentence on each.

4. Write a paragraph to explain how NICVA helps organisations within the voluntary and community sector.

NGO 2
AMNESTY INTERNATIONAL

Amnesty International is a campaigning organisation, made up of ordinary people from across the world. The people who support Amnesty come from many different faiths, cultures and backgrounds, but they all have one thing in common – a desire to stand up for human rights and to protect people who are denied justice, fairness, freedom and truth. Amnesty International is independent of any government, political party or religion.
Its website is: **www.amnesty.org.uk**

History

Peter Benenson was an English Lawyer who was concerned that people were being detained in prisons throughout the world because of their political or religious beliefs. In 1961 he wrote a significant newspaper article, 'The Forgotten Prisoners', calling for an international campaign to protest against this denial of human rights. It was intended to be a short appeal, but developed into a permanent international movement.

Amnesty International has grown into one of the largest and most respected voluntary organisations in the world, with 2.2 million members world wide and supporters from over 150 countries.

Vision, Mission and Values

Amnesty International's vision and mission
Amnesty International's vision is of a world in which every person enjoys all of the human rights enshrined in the Universal Declaration of Human Rights and other international human rights instruments. In pursuit of this vision, Amnesty International's mission is to undertake research and action focused on preventing and ending grave abuses of these rights.

Amnesty International's core values
Amnesty International forms a global community of human rights defenders based on the principles of international solidarity, effective action for the individual victim, global coverage, the universality

and indivisibility of human rights, impartiality and independence, and democracy and mutual respect.

Amnesty International's methods
Amnesty International addresses governments, intergovernmental organisations, armed political groups, companies and other non-state actors. Amnesty International seeks to expose human rights abuses accurately, quickly and persistently.

The work
In the early days, Amnesty International was concerned with prisoners of conscience; people denied their right to freedom because of their beliefs. Amnesty's work has grown and developed over the years to include other areas of concern. However, campaigning for everyone's human rights to be protected and respected is still at the heart of what they do. Amnesty believes human rights abuses anywhere in the world are the concern of all people and they work to improve people's lives through international solidarity.

These are some of the issues Amnesty International is currently concerned with:

- Women's rights, including violence against women.
- Children's rights.
- Campaigning to end torture.
- Campaigning to have the death penalty abolished.
- Promoting the rights of refugees and ensuring they have an adequate standard of living.
- The rights of prisoners of conscience.
- Dealing with human rights issues surrounding security and terrorism.
- To end the recruitment and use of child soldiers.
- Poverty and human rights.
- Campaigning to bring the arms trade under control.

Amnesty International has two main ways of working to achieve human rights for everyone:

1. **Promoting a general awareness of human rights:** This means making sure everyone agrees that human rights should be respected and supported, whether individuals, political parties,

or governments. An important part of Amnesty's work is producing educational materials for use in schools.

2. **Opposing specific abuses of human rights:** Amnesty carries out research in areas where it is thought human rights are being denied, and then produces detailed reports calling for action.

Sometimes Amnesty organises campaigns to mobilise public opinion, perhaps focussing on a particular country or issue. Letter writing is an effective technique that has been used since the early days of the organisation. These include protests and petitions to government officials, and letters of encouragement to prisoners of conscience. Amnesty International relies on volunteer action throughout the world, and writing letters is just one way to get involved with the organisation. Volunteers can play a vital role in many different areas, such as campaigning, working in a local office or fundraising.

--- Example: ---

AN EXAMPLE OF ONE OF AMNESTY'S CAMPAIGNS

Hakamada Iwao is believed to be the world's longest serving death row inmate. He was convicted after an unfair trial in 1968, principally on the basis of a confession extracted under duress, and which he later retracted.

To mark Hakamada Iwaos's 74th birthday Amnesty International UK called upon its supporters to take photographs of themselves holding up the message "Free Hakamada" to be sent to the Japanese embassy. They collected the many pictures they received and turned them into a giant birthday card.

On 10th March 2010, Hakamada Iwaos's birthday, a delegation from Amnesty International UK joined by Alistair Carmichael, Chair of the UK All Party Parliamentary Group against the Death Penalty, attended a meeting at the Japanese Embassy with the Political Secretary.

The delegation pressed for justice for Hakamada Iwao drawing attention to the circumstances of his original conviction, the amount of time

© Amnesty International

he has spent on death row and his mental health and handed over the birthday card as an expression of concern of people in the UK. The Political Secretary has promised to share our concerns with the Ambassador.

In April 2010, a cross-party group of parliamentary representatives in Japan joined together to campaign for the release of Hakamada Iwao. The group – called the Federation of Diet Members to Save Hakamada Iwao – is made up of 57 Diet (parliament) members of all parties, and is chaired by MAKINO Seishu, a member of the ruling Democratic Party of Japan (DPJ), representing Shizuoka Prefecture, where Hakamada Iwao was arrested.

On the 7th of May 2010, the group asked the Minister of Justice to immediately introduce of a moratorium on the execution of Hakamada Iwao. The Minister of Justice has said she has been concerned about this issue for a long time and is seriously considering the Federation's demand.

Amnesty International's Effectiveness

Peter Benenson's newspaper article, 'The Forgotten Prisoners', started a hugely influential campaigning organisation. Amnesty International has achieved worldwide success in raising awareness of human rights issues, whether in a primary school classroom or among world leaders. Amnesty has many success stories of prisoners who have been released through their campaigns but does not claim credit for these successes. However, many of the victims who have suffered human rights abuses often say that international pressure has led to their release and saved their lives.

1. Explain briefly how Amnesty International began.

2. Use the Internet to research the effectiveness of Amnesty International in promoting Human Rights in Rwanda.

3. What methods does Amnesty use to carry out its work?

Role Play

STREET CHILDREN

Background

In Honduras, there are thought to be around 7,500 street children, the majority living in cities such as the capitol, Tegucigalpa. These children live rough with no-one to care for them. They search through rubbish bins for food, or else they steal. Some of them abuse solvents. The authorities consider these children to be a nuisance and an embarrassment. Death squads, often thought to involve the local police, go out and shoot these children as a way of getting rid of them.

Newsflash!

Death squads struck again last night. A spokesperson from an international human rights organisation reported that masked men opened fire on a group of street children, killing five youngsters. The mayor has ordered a full enquiry to be set up …

The enquiry

At the enquiry, the following people are present, each with their point of view:

- **Police officer** – These children are criminals. They threaten members of the public and steal food. We need to get rid of them!

- **Local shopkeeper** – I cannot make ends meet. The children steal from my shop or else they frighten my customers away.

- **Tourist** – I feel sorry for the children and I think the authorities ought to do something. They frighten me though; a lady at my hotel had her bag snatched yesterday.

- **Human rights worker** – These children have no option but to steal, and these killings are murder. It is time society took responsibility for them!

- **Street child** – Nobody cares for us, so we care for each other. The streets are our only home. We have the same rights as everyone else!

Work in groups of six, with each person in the group taking on one of the roles above. One person should play the part of the mayor. Role play the enquiry, with each person taking a turn to represent their view.

DISCUSSION
What should be done to help the street children?

NGO 3
FRIENDS OF THE EARTH

Friends of the Earth operate on a local, national and global level. They campaign for solutions to environmental problems and in doing so, aim to make life better for everyone.
Their website is: **www.foe.co.uk**

History

Since 1971, FoE have been making things happen. Some big, some small. Like:

- Getting a grip on climate change.
- Laws to bring recycling to your doorstep.
- Warmer, more energy efficient homes.
- Protecting our countryside.
- Keeping genetically modified food off the menu.
- Persuading big companies to behave better.

What they're famous for

Dumping 1,500 non-returnable bottles outside Schweppes headquarters to make a statement about recycling.

Schweppes didn't want recycling. FoE did. FoE won in the end.

Their make up

Friends of the Earth is:

- the UK's most influential environmental campaigning organisation.
- the most extensive environmental network in the world, with almost 1 million supporters across five continents and more than 70 national organisations worldwide.
- a unique network of campaigning local groups, working in over 200 communities throughout England, Wales and Northern Ireland.
- dependent on individuals for over 90% of its income.

The big picture

FoE want a healthy planet and a good life for everyone on it.

They think they'll get it by persuading the government and the economy to give people a fair deal.

Vision, Mission and Values

Friends of the Earth stands for three big ideas:

- **There is a tomorrow**
  We need to use the planet like there is a tomorrow. This means living within the limits of the natural world.

- **Everyone gets a fair share**
  Everyone, everywhere, now and tomorrow, deserves to have a good life.

- **Change the rules**
  We need to change the rules so that the economy works for people and the environment, not pit one against the other.

Friends of the Earth seeks to influence the government to make changes to policies in favour of people and planet. It's not just what they do but the way they do it. FoE raise the issues but they also realise that to make things happen they need to:

- **Focus on the solution**
  FoE look for better alternatives to what's already out there.
- **Back it up with facts**
  FoE base everything on credible research.
- **Get lots of people involved**
  FoE make it easy for you to act.
- **Use their network**
  FoE have access to over 70 Friends of the Earth international groups and over 200 local groups in the UK.

The Campaigns

FoE is currently involved in the following campaigns:

- **Saving the planet** – Campaigning to protect the world's wildlife habitats. Friends of the Earth believe it is a priority to reduce factory farming, have better recycling facilities and to protect the world's forests.

- **Climate change** – Fighting climate change, through promoting green energy and opposing nuclear power.

- **Fair future** – Campaigning for rights and justice. This issue concerns the UK's planning laws and the public's right to have a greater involvement.

- **Smart economy** – Campaigning for a strong, green economy. Friends of the Earth believe that it need not be expensive to 'go green'. The government should act responsibly to make it cheaper and easier for families to have energy efficient homes with renewable technology.

- **Local action** – Campaigning on a local and regional level. Friends of the Earth have many local groups, encouraging people to take an interest in environmental issues. There are many ways to get involved, such as supporting a campaign, fundraising, delivering leaflets and lobbying MPs.

NEWS ITEM

DYING FOR A SNACK? YOU COULD BE KILLING THE ORANGUTAN!

Palm oil is an ingredient in many processed foods and household products, including chocolate, margarine, bread, toothpaste and detergents. It is a very cheap and useful cooking oil, and the plant itself is incredibly productive.

So what's the problem with palm oil? The issue is that palm oil production is threatening many endangered species, such as tigers and orangutans, with extinction. Rainforests are being cleared to make way for plantations and processing plants, destroying habitats and increasing CO_2 emmissions. Furthermore, it is unsustainable, with 3% of the world's palm oil coming from a sustainable source.

It also poses a threat to local people. In January 2010, people started to be removed from their homes in the Lacandon Jungle in Mexico. They were evicted without warning and prevented from taking any belongings with them. These evictions took place to make way for a palm oil processing plant, destroying precious conservation areas in the process. Friends of the Earth have launched a campaign, calling on people to email the Mexican President in protest.

DISCUSSION

From reading the News Item opposite discuss what you think should be done in the Lacandon Jungle:

- Would you consider supporting the FoE campaign?
- Or do you think the new processing plant should go ahead, as we need palm oil for so many products.
- Another consideration might be whether palm oil production could bring jobs to the area.

Friends of the Earth in Northern Ireland

Here are some examples of FoE's local campaigns and success stories:

Friends of the Earth
Northern Ireland

- **Environmental protection** – Northern Ireland has the least protected environment in the UK and Ireland. However, in 1996 FoE successfully campaigned to save Ballynahone bog in Co Londonderry from destruction by the Bulrush peat company. In 2005, FoE launched a campaign to review the way Northern Ireland's environment is protected. A report published in 2008 showed massive public support for this campaign. The work still continues.

- **Pollution** – Everyday untreated sewage is pumped directly into our rivers, loughs and seas. FoE has complained to the European court of justice and Northern Ireland Water is now investing in a new programme of sewerage works.

- **Rubbish dumping** – Northern Ireland is turning into a tip! Unlicensed sites throughout the countryside are being used for chemical waste, abandoned cars and animal carcasses. FoE is campaigning for a more effective policy for Northern Ireland.

- **Energy** – The coal-fired power station at Kilroot produces 20% of Northern Ireland's CO_2 emissions – yet we have great potential for both wind and wave power. FoE has successfully lobbied local politicians to sign an agreement to cut CO_2 emissions over a number of years.

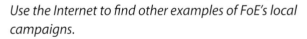

CHECK YOUR LEARNING

1. In your own words, write a paragraph to sum up what Friends of the Earth is trying to achieve.

2. Choose three examples of Friends of the Earth's campaigns which you think are the most important. Explain your choices.

3. What methods do Friends of the Earth use to try and get its message across?

ACTIVITY

Use the Internet to find other examples of FoE's local campaigns.

- Have they been successful?
- If so, why do you think these campaigns have been effective?

DISCUSSION

WHERE DO YOU STAND?

Here are some issues on which Friends of the Earth take a stand:

1. It is important for everyone to recycle as much as they can.
2. We do not need nuclear power – it is dangerous and expensive.

3. Everyone must try to reduce CO_2 emissions – try walking instead of using the car.
4. People need to be aware about energy efficiency at home and try to use renewable sources.
5. Say "No" to genetically modified food – it is bad for us and the environment.
6. We must support campaigns to stop the destruction of the world's forests.
7. Factory farming is bad for the environment. We could try eating less meat!
8. Everyone needs to be concerned that species of wildlife are becoming extinct.
9. We must find alternatives to fossil fuels, such as coal and oil.
10. Large companies must be more responsible and less concerned about profits.

Where do you stand on these issues?

Organise a 'Four Corners Debate' for your class. A different response is allocated to each corner of the room. As you hear each statement read out, stand in the area that represents your view. You may be asked to explain why you have chosen a particular corner.

AGREE	DEPENDS ON THE SITUATION
UNDECIDED	DISAGREE

OXFAM

Oxfam is a development agency involved in many issues worldwide, from climate change to conflict, and gender equality to the global economic crisis. However, all of these can be linked to one factor – poverty. Oxfam's work is all about fighting poverty, both at home and overseas. As Oxfam has been doing this for over 60 years, it is one of the most experienced and respected aid agencies in the world.
Their website is **www.oxfam.org.uk**

History

Oxfam started in 1942 as the **Oxford Committee for Famine Relief**. The group was begun by a University Vicar, Canon Milford, to help families whose lives had been destroyed by the Second World War. In towns across the UK, people collected parcels of food and clothes to send overseas.

The first of many charity shops was opened in Oxford in 1948 and today the shop network raises millions of pounds. Oxfam has always been active in the fight against poverty and has organised many campaigns to governments, international organisations and corporations. Oxfam believes it is important to work in partnership and **Oxfam International** was formed in 1995. In 1998 Oxfam Ireland, which is based in Belfast and Dublin, became an independent affiliate within Oxfam International. Independent Oxfam groups from 14 different countries work together to have an even greater global impact.

In 2005, the **Oxjam** music festival was started by a shop volunteer in Bangor, Co Down, to help fight poverty with music and appeal to younger people; the initiative has since spread throughout the world. One of the latest initiatives is **TRAILTREKKER**, in which contestants can build a team to tackle a charity challenge to walk a 100km route by day and night. Oxfam Ireland's TRAILTREKKER starts in the Mourne Mountains of County Down and ends in the Cooley Peninsula at Carlingford, County Louth.

Oxfam have a more detailed – and illustrated – history on their website (www.oxfam.org.uk), called 'The unconventional story of a unique organisation'. There's also a quiz on Oxfam and an eye-opening section called 'Reshaping the world'. It's worth a visit!

Vision, Mission and Values

The following information has been taken from Oxfam's Website:

Why fight poverty?

It's a basic question, but a good one. Why does Oxfam bother? Why put so much energy into saving lives, campaigning for change, and developing projects to give people more control over their future?

The answer is basic too. Belief – belief that in a wealthy world poverty is unjustifiable, and can be prevented. Belief that injustice must be challenged. And belief that with the right help, poor people themselves can change their lives for the better, for good. Believe it – then achieve it.

Everyone has the right to a life worth living – and to the basic things that make one possible. This belief shapes everything Oxfam does.

The Work

Oxfam fights poverty in three ways:

- **Campaigning for change** – Poverty isn't just about lack of resources. In a wealthy world it's about bad decisions made by powerful people. Oxfam campaigns hard, putting pressure on leaders for real lasting change.
- **Development work** – Poor people can take control, solve their own problems, and rely on themselves – with the right support. Fighting poverty, Oxfam funds long-term work worldwide.
- **Emergency response** – People need help in an emergency – fast. Oxfam saves lives, swiftly delivering aid, support and protection, and helps people prepare for future crises.

Below are just some of the issues Oxfam is currently concerned with; for a full list, see their website.

- **Climate change** – Rich countries produce most of the greenhouse gases that cause climate change. Yet, it's the poorest countries that are being hit hardest. More frequent and unpredictable droughts, floods, hunger and disease – this is the future for people living in poverty.
- **Conflict and natural disasters** – Every year, more than 35 million people have to abandon their homes as a result of war, crime, political unrest, and natural disaster. Many lose everything they own. And it's the world's poorest people who are hit hardest.
- **Debt and aid** – Two big issues seriously affect poor countries' chances of beating poverty. One is the amount of aid they get. The other is the amount of debt they repay. Across the world, impoverished countries are being forced to repay debts far bigger than original loans, instead of spending precious cash on essentials like schools and hospitals. Making sure developing countries get the aid money they need is just as important as cancelling their unpayable debts.

- **Trade** – Rich countries dominate the World Trade Organisation (the WTO), which agrees the way countries should trade. And they set rules under which poor countries continually lose out.

Success Stories

These are some examples of the many success stories which show Oxfam's effectiveness:

Cancelling Haiti's debt: Oxfam worked in partnership with other organisations and collected over 415,000 signatures on a petition requesting that Haiti's debt to the international community be cancelled. This will speed Haiti's recovery from the 2010 earthquake. In February 2010 seven of the world's wealthiest nations signed a pledge to cancel Haiti's debt.

Starbucks and Ethiopian coffee: In 2007, Oxfam supported Ethiopian coffee growers to get recognition for the premium coffee names that they produce. Oxfam's high profile campaign secured a fairer price for the farmers from the giant coffee chain, Starbucks.

MAKE POVERTY HISTORY: In 2005 Oxfam was one of the leading organisations in the biggest ever anti-poverty movement, under the MAKEPOVERTYHISTORY banner, calling for urgent action for more and better aid, debt cancellation and trade justice. Millions of people wore white bands, 444,000 people emailed the Prime Minister about poverty and 225,000 took to the streets of Edinburgh for the Make Poverty History march and rally. A 2005 summit of the 8 richest nations in the developed world (the G8 countries) signalled an extra $48 billion a year by 2010. $1billion per year of debt was dropped for 18 of the most highly indebted poor countries.

ACTIVITY

Organise an 'Action Week' in school where you focus on the work of one of the NGOs you have studied. In groups discuss which activities you think would be most effective. You could choose Oxfam, for example, and carry out some of the following activities:

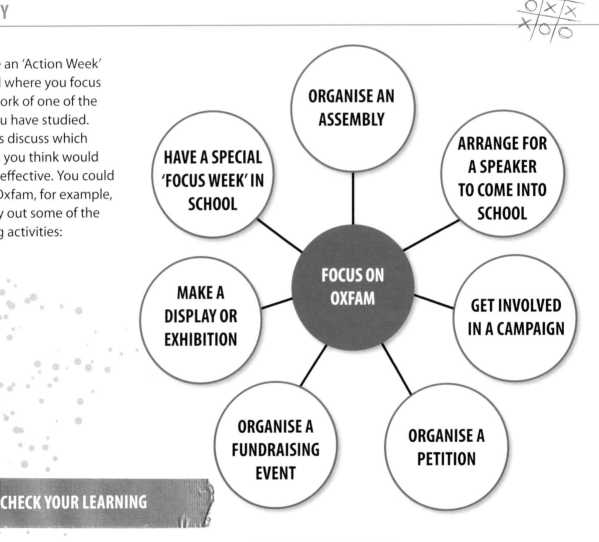

FOCUS ON OXFAM
- ORGANISE AN ASSEMBLY
- ARRANGE FOR A SPEAKER TO COME INTO SCHOOL
- GET INVOLVED IN A CAMPAIGN
- ORGANISE A PETITION
- ORGANISE A FUNDRAISING EVENT
- MAKE A DISPLAY OR EXHIBITION
- HAVE A SPECIAL 'FOCUS WEEK' IN SCHOOL

CHECK YOUR LEARNING

1. Why does Oxfam believe it is important to fight poverty?
2. Using the Internet, research to what extent Oxfam has been successful in reducing global poverty.
3. Explain how each of the following can have especially serious consequences for people living in poverty:
   - climate change
   - natural disasters
   - re-paying debts

EXTENSION TASK

Write a paragraph to sum up how effective you consider Oxfam's work to be.
In your answer you could consider the following points:

- The length of time Oxfam has been working.
- They operate at both national and international levels.
- Their success stories.
- In your opinion, is their publicity and fundraising effective? (What did you know about Oxfam before reading this book?)

SAVE THE CHILDREN

 Save the Children

Save the Children works in more than 120 countries, saving children's lives, fighting for their rights and helping them fulfill their potential. The charity's main focus is on the 8 million children under five who die every year from preventable causes. These children are dying in the world's poorest countries, from basic illnesses like diarrhoea and pneumonia. Save the Children helps to save lives directly through simple solutions like vaccinations, and also campaigns to persuade governments to stop children dying. Their website is: **www.savethechildren.org.uk**

History

The Save the Children Fund was established in London in 1919, following the turmoil of the First World War. Eglantyne Jebb and her sister Dorothy Buxton decided to act after seeing reports of children in appalling conditions. They started campaigning and raising money to help those children and others suffering the effects of war and poverty.

Save the Children quickly became known as a highly effective relief agency, able to provide food, clothing and money quickly and inexpensively. For example, during the 1921 famine in Russia, the organisation was able to mount an operation to feed 650,000 people – for a shilling per person per week.

Eglantyne Jebb wanted to make the rights and welfare of children a major issue around the world. Her 'Declaration of the Rights of the Child' inspired the present UN convention on the Rights of the Child. There are now 29 Save the Children member organisations operating all over the world.

The Work

Save the Children helps to save millions of children's lives through its work on the ground. It is also campaigning to persuade world leaders to prioritise saving children's lives.

It helps children get vaccinated against potentially deadly diseases. It helps them get lifesaving treatment when they're ill. It helps them get the food they need to survive, grow up healthy and have the chance to fulfil their potential. It focuses on the first five years – the time when children are most vulnerable.

Over the next three years, Save the Children plans to:

- Stop 3 million children dying from avoidable illnesses like pneumonia, diarrhoea and malaria.

- Train 50,000 healthworkers – nurses, and midwives and community workers – so that many more children can be vaccinated, diagnosed quickly and treated effectively.

- Make sure that 640,000 babies are delivered safely by skilled birth attendants trained by Save the Children. They will also provide essential postnatal care, getting newborn babies safely through those crucial first few weeks.

- Help at least 300,000 children suffering from severe malnutrition get the treatment they need and help 3 million children eat better, more nutritious food, so they're not in danger of becoming malnourished.

- Continue to respond quickly and effectively to save children's lives when disasters like floods or earthquakes strike.

Save the Children believes that every child should get the chance to fulfil their potential, so it is helping children in the UK too. Children living in poverty in the UK often grow up without the things most of us take for granted, like a warm home, the right food, and a good education. So Save the Children helps children here get a better start in life, and campaigns to make sure our government is working towards a time when no child in this country is born without a chance.

CASE STUDY: MALARIA

Eight-month-old Jenny with her mother being diagnosed at Suehn Clinic, Liberia. She was diagnosed with malaria, a big killer of children under the age of five in Africa. Save the Children is supporting clinics like this to help save children's lives.

CASE STUDY: HUNGER

Jihad from Bangladesh is only ten weeks old, but he has already had surgery to stop him vomiting because he was so malnourished. Now he is slowly improving. Nearly half of all children under five in Bangladesh are under-weight or small for their age as a result of malnutrition.

CASE STUDY: INFANT AND MATERNAL MORTALITLY

Bintu, a Maternal and Child Health Aid at Kroo Bay clinic, Freetown, Sierra Leone, examines Mabinti Kamara, who's eight months pregnant.

Freetown has the world's worst infant and maternal mortality rates. One in 4 children die before they reach the age of 5 and one in 6 mothers dies during child birth (in the UK, the rate is one in 3,800).

The Kroo Bay Community Health Centre has a catchment area of over 8,000 people but lacks adequate facilities to provide even basic care, without basics such as bedpans, surgical spirits and cotton wool. It has no electricity and clean drinking water must be fetched from the nearby well everyday. Save the Children is working in this area by training volunteer health workers, for additional care in the community.

CASE STUDY: DIARRHOEA

Ashraf, 4 months, is suffering from diarrhoea, his aunt Razia is taking him to Save the Children's mobile health clinic in Holumbi Kalan, a slum in north west Delhi, for treatment. Ashraf's mother, Alia, is at home sick so is unable to take him herself. At the clinic Ashraf is treated by Dr Anita Harish and given medication.

Alia, his mother, says that, "coming to the mobile health clinic has been beneficial because we now get free medication and we don't have to travel too far for the treatment. We get comfort quickly, and this is why it helps".

Pneumonia and diarrhoea kill almost three times more under-fives than malaria and HIV combined, amounting to over 4,000 a day for pneumonia and nearly the same for diarrhoea.

Responding to an emergency

A natural disaster, such as a flood or earthquake, can happen without warning. Thousands of people can be killed and many more left homeless or without food, water or healthcare. Save the Children is a worldwide network, so if there is a disaster it can respond quickly to save lives and help families to cope.

An emergency response on a large scale usually involves 4 steps:

1. **Preparation and training** – Save the Children trains staff to respond quickly and efficiently if there is an emergency. It also works with local communities to help them prepare for a possible disaster.

2. **Immediate help** – Save the Children teams, working with local partners, try to reach the area as soon as possible. They make sure that essential relief supplies are available, such as water, food, blankets and temporary shelters.

3. **Full-scale relief effort** – After a disaster, Save the Children begins to assess the problem and plan how to respond. In a large-scale emergency it may be necessary to fly in specialist help and extra supplies. When a disaster strikes, children

are often separated from their parents and are especially vulnerable. Save the Children tries to reunite families so children can be protected.

4. **Helping children and families rebuild their lives** – It is especially important for children to have a sense of normality, even in difficult circumstances. Save the Children provides temporary schools and a safe place to play. After an emergency, Save the Children helps people to rebuild their lives. This might mean giving a family money to re-start a business or build a new home.

Example:

The following example shows how Save the Children has responded in an emergency situation:

"In January 2010, a huge earthquake struck the island of Haiti. Save the Children responded immediately, making sure that injured children got life-saving treatment, and that those who were separated from their families were cared for and reunited where possible. In the year after the earthquake, we have helped more than half a million children, fighting the cholera outbreak, providing clean water and food and giving children the chance to get back to school and start the rest of their lives."

How to help

There are a number of ways in which the public can get involved and help Save the Children carry out their work:

- **Support a campaign** – Save the Children is asking people to join its No Child Born to Die campaign. Supporters can get involved by doing what they're born to do e.g. if they're 'born to run' they can join a Save the Children running group. It also regularly asks people to sign petitions by email asking the government to act to help children.

- **Fundraise** – Save the Children week takes place each spring. It is a great opportunity to help raise vital funds; £10 can help to treat 50 babies with life-threatening diarrhoea. If a young child is under-nourished and there is no clean drinking water or medical help available, diarrhoea can be fatal. However, it is cheap and easy to cure with the right treatment.

- **Donate** – Money is always a welcome donation, but so are items for Save the Children's shops.

- **Go shopping** – Save the children has over 120 shops across the UK selling both new and second hand goods.

- **Recycle** – Making an effort to recycle can help to save children's lives. Donating your old mobile phone or empty ink cartridges can help raise money.

- **Volunteer** – There are a number of opportunities for voluntary work, from fundraising to campaigning, and the shops are mainly staffed by volunteer workers.

- **Companies and trusts** – Companies can make a big difference to many children by funding one of Save the Children's projects.

Save the Children's effectiveness

Save the Children aims to change the lives of children for the better – and they are achieving this. Some reasons for their success include:

- It is well-established and has been operating for over 90 years.

- It is part of a worldwide network.

- It believes in campaigning and working with partners to make an even bigger impact.

CHECK YOUR LEARNING

1. Describe the main focus of this NGO.
2. Give examples of how Save the children raise the money needed to carry out their work.
3. Give examples of how Save the Children responds in an emergency situation.

EXTENSION TASK

Visit the Save the Children website: www.savethechildren.org.uk

- Go to 'Where we work' and read the information about the UK.

- Write an article for a newspaper, giving facts about child poverty in the UK and highlighting some of the ways in which Save the Children is addressing the situation. You could end your report with a personal comment on what further action is needed.

QUIZ: DEALING WITH DISASTERS – WHAT WOULD YOU DO?

Imagine you are part of a disaster response team which has to make rapid decisions about issues which affect survivors.

Read each of the decisions below and decide whether each one is right or wrong.

1. As soon as you receive news of the disaster you send out an urgent appeal for international assistance from doctors, nurses and other medical staff.

2. Through the press and TV, you ask people in the UK not to collect or send medicines, clothing or equipment.

3. The top priority must be gathering and disposing of dead bodies because they are a danger of infection and disease.

4. It is best to house people as close as possible to their own homes, rather than in resettlement camps.

5. Food is a top priority after a major disaster, otherwise people will starve.

6. Where there are limited food supplies, the young and the old should be given food first.

7. When disaster strikes, individual team members who live in the area should take care of their own family and belongings first.

8. You ask the Police and the army to guard homes, shops and factories. This will stop people from stealing things when the owners are not there.

9. Even weeks after a disaster you must expect things to be far from back to normal. Most services will not be running properly.

10. The disaster will have focussed the world's attention on the plight of the people you have been helping. If a disaster happens here again, it will be easier to raise the resources you need. The disaster will not have such a devastating effect.

DISCUSSION

Once you have written down your answers, discuss them in groups of 4 and compare them to the answers listed in the box below.

You might not necessarily agree with all the answers given below. If so justify *your* answers to the rest of your group.

ANSWERS

1. **Wrong** – Local health services are normally able to cope in case of disaster. People from the area can speak the local language and are familiar with the local culture and environment. They know what health services already exist and how to use them. Foreign teams may provide specialist skills and equipment, but they have to be fed and housed.

2. **Right** – It is important that the wrong items are not sent. Disaster-relief teams do not want to be occupied with sorting out items that can or cannot be used. Concerned people in Britain should wait to hear exactly what is needed, or should give money to agencies so that the right materials can be bought.

3. **Wrong** – Bodies do not cause epidemics, or transmit diseases during the first seventy-two hours after death. The top priority is rescuing and caring for the injured.

4. **Right** – Keeping people as close as possible to their homes is the best option. Settlement camps are a last resort, since they have problems of their own. Illness can spread more easily if people are living in cramped conditions, and psychologically it is better for people to stay in their own environment, if possible. International help in the form of building materials and tools may be needed, however.

5. **Right** – Food is a top priority after a flood or a hurricane, but it should be stored and given out properly. After the disaster, giving seeds and tools so that people can grow their own food is important.

6. **Wrong** – Food should be given to everyone. People who are involved in rescuing and rebuilding work (not usually the youngest or eldest) need a regular food supply so that they can continue working.

7. **Wrong** – Although it is understandable that individuals will wish to take care of their own families first, teamwork is very important in a disaster. Sometimes teams can be trained beforehand so that each person knows what they should do.

8. **Wrong** – The media often report that selfish behaviour is common after a disaster. In fact, disaster situations usually bring out the best in people. Communities join together to deal with difficult situations. The police and the army will be needed to help with the rescue and rebuilding.

9. **Right** – Long after a disaster has disappeared from the headlines, people are still coping with its effects. The damage may last many years. Health and water supplies may be destroyed. Rebuilding is very costly.

10. **Wrong** – Unfortunately the world's attention span is very limited. The media soon lose interest. You may be able to raise some funds for long-term recovery, but it will be difficult to make sure that people are not vulnerable to the next disaster.

Source: http://www.oxfam.org.uk/education/resources/dealing_disasters/files/lesson3_when_disaster_strikes.pdf
Adapted by the publisher from 'Dealing with Disasters, Lesson Plan 3: Disaster Strikes', 2007-2008, with the permission of Oxfam GB, Oxfam House, John Smith Drive, Cowley, Oxford OX4 2JY, UK www.oxfam.org.uk/education. Oxfam GB does not necessarily endorse any text or activities that accompany the materials, nor has it approved the adapted text.

NEWS ITEM

AGENCIES HELP QUAKE RESCUE EFFORT

Emergency crews, charities and the UK government are co-ordinating efforts to help with the rescue operation in Haiti after it was hit by an earthquake. The 7.0-magnitude quake that hit south of the Haitian capital Port-au-Prince is feared to have killed thousands of people across the Caribbean country.

Mobilising support

Save the Children, which has 60 staff working in Haiti, has released £50,000, launching an appeal for £3m.

Oxfam said it had a 100-strong team focusing on public health, water and sanitation services to prevent the spread of waterborne disease in Haiti. It has launched an appeal for millions of pounds.

Source: http://news.bbc.co.uk/go/pr/fr/-/1/hi/uk/8457660.stm

RESEARCH ACTIVITY

Oxfam and Save the Children both respond to emergency situations as an important part of their work. Use the NEWS ITEM and the Internet to research the following:

- After the Haiti earthquake, what action was taken by each of these organisations?

- Use the websites below to find out more information about their emergency response. Write a brief account in your folder or notebook.

  http://www.savethechildren.org.uk/en/10181.htm

  http://www.oxfam.org.uk/oxfam_in_action/emergencies/haiti-earthquake.html

NGO 6

WAR ON WANT NI

War on Want NI was Northern Ireland's first international development agency, and for 50 years has supported some of the most disadvantaged communities in Africa. It raises funds to support this work from its 13 retail shops, from general fundraising and from Statutory and non-statutory funders.

Their website is: **www.waronwantni.org**

History

For 50 years War on Want NI has been fighting poverty and inequality for some of the poorest people in the world.

War on Want NI was established in 1961 during the "Golden Years" of European economic prosperity. Financial stability led to a decade of discovery in the 1960s; this created a generation who began questioning the inequalities and injustices in the world.

The primary aim of War on Want NI was to spark public consciousness to the fact that two-thirds of mankind was suffering from malnutrition and to create public opinion that would encourage more governmental aid towards the relief of poverty.

In Northern Ireland, War on Want NI immediately began raising awareness and funding for poverty alleviation programmes. Within 18 months, the first War on Want NI shop opened in Bradbury Place, Belfast.

The vision that established War on Want NI 50 years ago remains true today. War on Want NI is dedicated to global education and advocacy work in the hope that someday poverty will become a thing of the past.

Aims, Vision and Mission

The following information comes from the War on Want NI website:

Aims

- Overseas Rural Livelihood Security Programme
- Home based Global Education
- Home based Advocacy and Campaigning

Mission

- To alleviate poverty by working in partnership with organisations representing poor communities in developing countries, and challenging the systems that keep them poor.

Vision

- War on Want NI's vision is of a world where everyone has access to the resources they need to achieve their full potential.

The Work

How does War on Want NI try to achieve their aims, vision and mission?

Raising awareness and lobbying at home

At home War on Want NI raises awareness of poverty issues among school pupils and other interested groups. In Global Education sessions groups are encouraged to explore the causes and effects of poverty and how they, in this part of the world, can contribute to the eradication of poverty.

Working within Non-government Organisations' umbrella organisations such as Dochas and CADA, War on Want NI works with elected representatives and other decision makers to bring about change for the betterment of poor people in the developing world.

Poverty alleviation programmes in Africa

War on Want NI's main goal is to help people help themselves out of poverty. To this extent, War on Want NI works with local non-government and community based organisations to implement lasting solutions to specific economic and social problems in their community.

War on Want NI works in partnership with organisations representing and helping vulnerable people and their communities develop participatory and sustainable programmes that will improve their quality of life. Through these programmes, individuals are able to earn an income that will feed their families and cover basic essentials such as education and medicine.

Through active input from these partners and other key stakeholders, War on Want NI has developed individual country strategies in Uganda, Malawi and Tanzania. War on Want NI focuses on the most cost effective programmes that offer secure, sustainable livelihoods that can operate within the governments' existing poverty reduction frameworks.

War on Want NI provides financial and non-financial resources to their partners and their War on Want NI staff in Africa work on the ground providing skills and training programmes for each partner group to ensure that each partner's project is reaching its full potential.

War on Want NI's support reflects local issues such as gender equality, the impact of HIV/Aids on a community, climate change and other environmental issues. This comprehensive approach brings out the strengths of each community and allows individuals to become entrepreneurs of their own livelihood.

ACTIVITY

IN THE HOT SEAT

Imagine you are a fundraiser for War on Want NI.

- Choose one of War on Want NI's projects in Africa.
- Imagine that the rest of your class are wealthy business people who want to support a good cause.
- What would you say to convince them to support your project?
- They might put you 'in the hot seat' and ask you some tricky questions. You need to be sure of your facts!

How you can help

War on Want NI has a small staff of less than twenty based in Northern Ireland and over 350 volunteers, working hard to raise money for projects overseas. They are glad of any donated goods to be sold in their charity shops, and fundraising efforts are always appreciated. However, War on Want NI also has some original ways to raise money:

- **Buy a gift** – If you have a friend or family member who really does have everything, why not buy them a charity present that will help some of the poorest communities in Africa? Hens and chicks for one family cost £20, while £50 will buy a herd of five goats.

- **Book a fashion show** – War on Want NI is well known for their fashion shows – with a difference! Volunteer models stage a show of historical outfits from the 19th and 20th centuries.

- **Volunteer** – There are opportunities in charity shops, in the office in Belfast.

CHECK YOUR LEARNING

1. Explain in your own words how War on Want NI was started.

2. What activities does War on Want NI carry out in Northern Ireland?

3. Explain how War on Want NI works in partnership with community groups in Africa.

EXTENSION TASK

- Choose one of War on Want NI's African projects and visit their website to find out more about it.

- Write a report about how this project is making a difference in people's lives. The aim of your report is to convince people in Northern Ireland to give money to support this project.

CASE STUDY: MUHAMAID ISSA FROM MALAWI

Malawi's population is 15.3 million and over 90% live in rural areas. This means the majority of the population must rely on small plots of land that can only be farmed during the rainy season 6-9 months of the year. Consequently, more than half of its people live below the poverty line and women account for the majority of the population living below this line.

War on Want NI has been involved with poverty reduction projects in Malawi since 2004, and offers training and support for its local partners representing some of the poorest farmers. One of its objectives is to encourage farmers to install irrigation systems so food can be grown all year. Currently it is concentrating its work in the Machinga and Balaka districts of southern Malawi where poverty levels are higher than the country's average.

Muhamaid Issa lives in the Mpotola village in the Machinga district in south Malawi where she is one of 59 farmers who benefit from the Kachere irrigation scheme. To eradicate the annual food security problem in the village, environmental NGO Greenline helped the villagers improve their cultivation and irrigation methods. This allowed them to improve their growing area and cultivate in the rainy season confident that they already have sufficient food for many months.

This Mpotola farmers co-operated in a vulnerability study carried out by War on Want NI to provide information to improve its future work. This irrigated site has already made a huge boost to the living standard of the villagers and is attracting much attention from communities in the surrounding villages who would like to follow this example.

CASE STUDY:
ARIKO ROBERT FROM UGANDA

Omodio Amorican Farmers Association was formed in 2000 to address the problems of poverty and widespread food insecurity caused by the ongoing neighbouring Karamjong cattle rustling. War on Want NI have been supporting this community based group since 2003 and have seen it grow from strength to strength. Their activities have included livestock rearing, agricultural production, and most importantly construction of a grain store. Not only does the grain store provide a safe place to house their grinding mill and oil press, both of which add value to their agricultural produce as they can charge a fee for the service, but also it allows their crop to be stored after harvest when the prices are low so allowing the members the facility to delay the sale of their product until the market prices rise.

This dynamic group also set up a micro loan scheme amongst its members from which Mr Ariko Robert has benefited. Seeing the growth in the use of mobile phones in the area and no facility to charge the phones, Robert bought some very simple solar equipment with a loan of approximately £40 and has set up a small business charging mobile phones. This venture has not only given Robert some additional income but is also proving a great asset to the community. Given the remoteness of the village the local people are now able to call an ambulance in a medical emergency and have the security of being able to get help quickly in the event of an imminent cattle raid. In true entrepreneurial spirit the farmers are also able to quickly ascertain availability and price of their produce in the neighbouring market.

CASE STUDY:
ALFA NZUNDA
FROM TANZANIA

In 1998 Linda Ngido, a qualified special needs teacher, recognised the lack of provision for children and young people with learning difficulties and established The Mehayo Trust Fund in Morogoro Tanzania. In those early days poor families, unable to take care of a child with disabilities were as a last resort leaving their babies and young children at the centre. Now many of those children are becoming mature and the long term goal of the organisation is to create employment opportunities and independent sustainable living for young people with mental disabilities.

19 year old Alfa Nzunda has been attending the Mehayo centre as a day boy since 2001. Alfa was diagnosed as having Downs Syndrome and also has respiratory problems, which are improving with proper medical care. He is the youngest of 7 children and lives with his mother. Through the care and nurturing he has received at the centre Alfa has become a confident and responsible young man. His friendly disposition makes him popular with both staff and fellow pupils. He has learned weaving and enjoys making table mats which are sold locally with other young people's handicrafts to support the running costs of the centre.

DISCUSSION

1. Explain how Muhamaid Issa benefits from the Kachere irrigation scheme.

2. What are the priorities for the Omodio Amorican Farmers Association?

3. What do you think might have happened to Alfa Nzunda without the Mehayo Trust Fund?

FOR DISCUSSION

Consider the following quotation:

"There is enough on earth for everybody's need but not enough for anybody's greed."

Mahatma Gandhi

Do you agree that if everyone tried to be less selfish, then inequality and injustice would become things of the past?

Work in groups of about 4:

- Produce a large spider diagram or flowchart to show the causes and consequences of social inequality and injustice. For each issue on your diagram, write beside it which NGO is seeking to address the problem.

- Choose one of the NGOs studied in this section. Use their website to research their work further and produce a PowerPoint presentation to show to the rest of the class.

evaluation

Choose one of the NGOs you are studying. Evaluate how this organisation can have an effect on the lives of the people it is working with.

DISCUSSION

Read the following quotes.

"NGOs have a more important role to play in the developing world than in Northern Ireland."

"The public should not need to support NGOs in order to tackle injustice in the world – it is everyone's right to have a decent standard of living!"

Do you agree or disagree?

What evidence would you use to support your views?

EXAM FOCUS

Some questions testing the application of knowledge and understanding will need longer answers.

The following question will give you practice at this:

Read the source below and use it to help you answer this question.

(a) (i) Explain how an NGO can raise public awareness.

[2 marks]

    (ii) Explain what is meant by an NGO taking local action.

[2 marks]

(b) Explain how Friends of the Earth encourage the public to support their work.

[6 marks]

Source:

"Friends of the Earth campaigns on environmental issues such as climate change. It raises public awareness about the need for people to use energy more efficiently through the media. It encourages people to take action at a local, national and global level to reduce carbon emissions. Within their own communities people can do simple things to make a difference. These include switching off electrical appliances when they are not in use and turning down the thermostat. Using less energy will help stop climate change and is also very cost effective."

Source adapted from http://www.foe.co.uk/northern_ireland/campaigns/climate_index. html

INFORMATIO

The total mark
Quality of writ
Figures in brac
question or par

each

le

KEY DEMOCRATIC INSTITUTIONS AND THEIR ROLE IN PROMOTING INCLUSION, JUSTICE AND DEMOCRACY

CHAPTER SUMMARY

In this chapter you will be studying:

- The Good Friday Agreement and what it means to the citizens of Northern Ireland.
- The role of the Northern Ireland Assembly and the Executive Committee.
- How the Northern Ireland Human Rights Commission promotes equality and justice.
- The work of the Police Ombudsman's Office.

LIVING IN A DEMOCRACY

POWER TO THE PEOPLE!

Most people would agree that a democracy is one of the fairest types of government as it means that everyone is considered equal. A democracy should give equality and freedom to all citizens and everyone has equal access to power. People have the security of knowing that they can live in safety without fear of arrest because of their religious or political views.

The idea of democracy developed in Greece around 507 BCE. The term comes from two Greek words:

demos = people

kratos = power

A democracy is literally 'power to the people'. This probably sounds like potential chaos! After all, how can everyone have power and rule the country? Careful organisation is needed.

Allowing every individual to vote on every single law or issue would be difficult to organise, not to mention expensive. In most democratic countries, there is a government of representatives elected by the people. This is known as a representative democracy. The people choose someone to represent them by voting in an election. The representative becomes a member of the local council or a member of Parliament in the central Government. Their job is to speak on behalf of the community who has elected them and if necessary fight for their rights.

For some important decisions, all citizens are invited to vote. This is called a referendum. For example, in 1998 people in Northern Ireland were given the opportunity to vote for or against the Good Friday Agreement.

 In the UK, all citizens aged 18 years or over have the right to vote. Voting is important because it is a way for everyone to have their say in how a country is run. There is no point moaning about the government if you cannot be bothered to go out and vote!

"The ballot is stronger than the bullet."

Abraham Lincoln (1809–1865)

DISCUSSION
What does this mean? Do you agree?

CHARACTERISTICS OF A DEMOCRACY
Different countries will have their own democratic systems of government. However, there are some features that all democracies will have:

- All adult citizens can play a part in running their country by having a vote. Everyone has the right to use their vote freely to choose the person they think will best represent them.

- One of the main ideas behind a democracy is that of majority rule. This means that people vote for their leaders. Those who receive the most votes are trusted to make decisions on behalf of the people. In some democracies, where there is an important issue to be decided, the people will be asked to vote directly and the most popular choice will be followed.

- In a democracy, there will be a central government, responsible for decisions that affect the whole country. Power will also be shared out so some decisions can be made at a local level.

- One of the most important functions of a democracy is to protect the rights of everyone in the community. These include freedom of speech and religion, the right to be protected equally under the law and the right to play a full part in the political, economic and cultural life of society.

- The government of a democracy is elected by the people and it should also be accountable to the people. This means that if someone has a complaint about a government service or organisation, then they have the right to say what is wrong and for it to be investigated fairly.

VOTING IN NORTHERN IRELAND

In Northern Ireland, we can vote for **MPs** (to represent us at Westminster), **MEPs** (members of the European Parliament) and **MLAs** (members of the Northern Ireland Assembly). For Westminster elections, the voting system **First Past the Post** is used.* Each voter chooses one candidate and the one with the most votes wins the seat.

The other elections use **Proportional Representation**. Many people think this is a fairer system, as a wider spread of parties can take responsibility and every vote counts. If a party gets 50% of the total votes, for example, then they will get approximately 50% of the seats.

* *At the time of writing this is under review in Parliament, so the reader should check current practice.*

HOW DOES PR WORK?

- Voters do not pick one candidate, but choose as many as they like, writing '1' beside their first choice, '2' for the second choice, and so on. All the first choice votes are counted first.

- A quota is worked out, which depends on the number of seats and the number of valid votes.

- Once a candidate reaches the quota, any 'extra' votes are transferred to other candidates, according to the voters' stated preferences.

- If nobody reaches the quota, the votes for the candidate with the lowest number are transferred to other candidates, again according to the voters' stated preferences.

- The idea is to reduce the total number of candidates to the number of seats in a constituency. This is six for an Assembly election.

This system of PR is called the **Single Transferable Vote.**

Wordbox

CONSTITUENCY

A constituency is an area represented by a member of parliament (MP). The majority of people living in this area will have voted for this person the last time an election was held. Sometimes a constituency will be divided into smaller areas and there will be more than one MP representing the people.

DEMOCRACY GAMES
Visit www.demgames.org and try out the games below:
- Captain Campaign
- Councillor Quest

You can organise a political campaign or become a local councillor for a day.

NATIONAL, REGIONAL AND LOCAL GOVERNMENT

The government of a country is organised on different levels, so it can operate efficiently. You would expect the national government of a country to be responsible for the nation's security, but not for deciding when a local recycling centre should be open to the public. It is better for everyone if local decisions are made locally.

In Northern Ireland, government is organised in the following way:

National government: Decisions made by Parliament in Westminster affect people in Northern Ireland as part of the United Kingdom. For example, the annual budget drawn up by the Chancellor of the Exchequer applies to Northern Ireland, as do many of the laws that are passed in Westminster.

Regional government: The Northern Ireland Assembly has responsibility for issues that apply to the whole of Northern Ireland.

Local government: Local councils are responsible for matters concerning a smaller area, such as a town or district. In Northern Ireland, government at local level also includes Education and Library Boards who have responsibility for schools and education in a particular area.

National affairs, such as defence, foreign policy and taxation, are the responsibility of central government (national government). Local government is concerned with a particular area and looks after roads, education and housing. A local council is made up of elected councillors and paid officials. People vote for a councillor to represent their area and most of them are representatives of a political party. Local councils receive funding from the government and through rates, a local tax paid by householders. There are some duties which a local council has to carry out, such as rubbish collections and cleaning the streets. Other activities might depend on whether there is enough money available, such as putting on a firework display or organising an open air concert.

For the rest of this chapter you will be learning about the regional government of Northern Ireland.

ACTIVITY

DEMOCRACY IN ACTION

Have you ever thought you would like to go into politics? Now is your chance to try in a class election!

For this activity, you will work in a group of around 4 people.

- Imagine that your group is a political party. The first thing you need to do is decide on a name for yourself.

- Next, discuss what issues you think are important and what policies you will make.

- Write your **manifesto** – this is a document where you set out your beliefs and policies. Remember you must try to appeal to the voters, but you must also be realistic.

- You could also produce posters to help your campaign.

- Each group then elects a party leader. It will be the leader's responsibility to make a speech to the rest of the class about their party and why everyone should vote for them.

- Finally there is an election, where the class vote for the best party.

evaluation

Evaluate the role of democracy in society.

THE GOOD FRIDAY AGREEMENT

ON THE WAY TO A PEACEFUL NORTHERN IRELAND ...

The term **'Peace Process'** is often used when people are referring to Northern Ireland's recent history. It covers the events leading to the Provisional IRA ceasefire in 1994, the Good Friday agreement and the developments which have followed.

The **Good Friday Agreement** was considered to be a major political development in the peace process. The agreement was reached after multi-party negotiations had taken place. The 65 page document was signed in Belfast on 10th April 1998 (Good Friday) by the British and Irish governments.

The leaders of **Sinn Féin** and the **SDLP** welcomed the agreement. David Trimble, leader of the **Ulster Unionists**, was concerned about a party with paramilitary links holding office in the Northern Ireland Assembly before decommissioning (giving up weapons) had taken place. Prime Minister Tony Blair assured him this would not happen and that decommissioning would begin as soon as the new assembly was set up. The Ulster Unionists accepted the agreement, which left the **DUP** as the only large party to oppose the agreement.

The Good Friday Agreement was concerned with relationships:

- within Northern Ireland
- between Northern Ireland and the Republic of Ireland and
- between Northern Ireland and the rest of the UK

The next step was to see what the people of Northern Ireland thought of the Agreement. The final version was posted to every household in Northern Ireland and a **referendum** was held on 22nd May 1998. People could vote 'yes' or 'no' and the result was 71% in favour of the Good Friday Agreement. On the same day, people in the Republic of Ireland voted on whether they agreed to change their constitution in line with the agreement; 94% voted in favour of this.

The Northern Ireland Assembly was elected in June 1998. The Ulster Unionists won the largest share of the votes and took 28 seats. The SDLP won 24, with Sinn Féin taking 18 seats. The new government for Northern Ireland was formed, but did not yet have the power to rule.

On 1st December 1999 at midnight, the power to rule Northern Ireland passed from Westminster to Belfast. On 2nd December 1999, the Irish government removed its claim to Northern Ireland from its constitution. The Northern Ireland Assembly could now govern Northern Ireland and the new **Northern Ireland Executive** met for the first time.

The Good Friday Agreement was a historic breakthrough. It gave the chance of a new start for relationships within Northern Ireland, with the Republic of Ireland and the rest of the UK. The agreement gave people of Northern Ireland the choice of identifying themselves as Irish, British or both.

The Good Friday Agreement led to the passing of important new laws in the **Northern Ireland Act 1998**. In Chapter 3, you looked at the importance of **Section 75** in securing equality of opportunity for all people in Northern Ireland. The Agreement is based on the ideas of human rights, equality and mutual respect for all people, and working towards a tolerant and inclusive society. Under the Good Friday Agreement, the **Northern Ireland Human Rights Commission** started work on 1st March 1999. A **Bill of Rights** is promised for the people of Northern Ireland.

However, there have been a number of issues with the Good Friday Agreement, and it has not been easy to carry it out. Some of the issues have included:

- **Paramilitary prisoners** – These prisoners were to be released early if their organisations kept to the ceasefire. However, some people were unhappy about this.
- **The reform of the Police** – For many people, this was the most important issue as they felt the police force did not meet the needs of their local community.
- **Decommissioning of weapons** – Some parties complained that this was not happening fast enough.

As a result of these problems, The Northern Ireland Assembly and Executive Committee have had power for only limited periods of time between 1998 and 2007. During this period, power has been passed back to Westminster three times, the longest period being between 2002 and 2007.

A breakthrough was achieved on 13th October 2006, with the publication of the **St Andrews Agreement**. Talks were held at St Andrews in Scotland, between the British Prime Minister, Irish Taoiseach and Northern Ireland's political parties. The St Andrews Agreement set out a clear way forward for all parties to commit to a power-sharing government and to show their support for the police and criminal justice systems. The Northern Ireland Assembly and Executive were functioning again by early 2007.

DISCUSSION

- How does the Good Friday Agreement benefit the people of Northern Ireland?
- Why do you think this agreement has faced setbacks?
- What problems could be involved in upholding this agreement in the future?

Evaluate the impact of the Good Friday Agreement on the citizens of Northern Ireland.

THE NORTHERN IRELAND ASSEMBLY

WHAT IS THE NORTHERN IRELAND ASSEMBLY?

The Northern Ireland Assembly was established as part of the Good Friday Agreement. Northern Ireland remains part of the United Kingdom, but the agreement resulted in **devolution**, meaning that the responsibility for the day to day running of Northern Ireland is now carried out by Northern Ireland's politicians. The governing body is the Northern Ireland Assembly. The Assembly has full authority to pass laws and to make decisions on the work of Northern Ireland Government departments. There are 108 elected members* of the Legislative Assembly (MLAs) representing eight political parties. The Assembly meets in Parliament buildings in Stormont, Belfast twice a week. Members of the public are welcome to attend.

Wordbox

DEVOLUTION
This is a transfer of power from a higher level (such as the national government) to a lower level (such as the government of a particular region). Devolution can give regional governments greater responsibility in decision-making without the national government giving up its overall authority.

* At the time of writing the number of constituencies in Northern Ireland is under review, so the reader should check this figure.

WHEN DID THE ASSEMBLY TAKE POWER?

Following the referendum on the Good Friday Agreement, elections took place to choose the members of the New Assembly. The Single Transferable Vote System was used to ensure proportional representation. Six members were elected from each of Northern Ireland's constituencies. The New Northern Ireland Assembly first met in 'shadow' form (meaning it did not yet have the power to govern) on 1st July 1998. The New Assembly needed to have time to prepare for governing Northern Ireland. At midnight on 1st December 1999, full power was devolved to the Northern Ireland Assembly and the word 'new' was dropped from the name. On 6th December 1999, the first meeting of the Northern Ireland Assembly with devolved powers took place.

WHAT ARE THE RESPONSIBILITIES OF THE ASSEMBLY?

When the Northern Ireland Assembly was established, three areas of responsibility were created:

1. **Transferred matters** – Public services, such as education, health and agriculture.
2. **Reserved matters** – On-going police enquiries, Human Rights and Electoral Policy.
3. **Excepted matters** – Matters of national importance, such as defence, taxation and foreign policy.

The Assembly has full responsibility for all transferred matters. There is a minister responsible for each area and together they make up an Executive Committee, which has special powers within the Assembly. Reserved matters can be transferred to the Assembly at a later date; however, the Assembly could take responsibility for these matters with the Secretary of State's consent. Excepted matters remain the responsibility of the United Kingdom Parliament.

HOW DOES THE ASSEMBLY CARRY OUT ITS WORK?

The Assembly carries out its work through meetings and committees:

- **Plenary meetings** – These are the weekly meetings (usually held on Mondays and Tuesdays) in the Assembly Chamber at Stormont.

- **Statutory Committees** – Ten Committees were established under the Northern Ireland Act 1998, each one shadowing a government department at Stormont, such as education or agriculture.

The St Andrews Agreement led to the Committee for the Office of the First Minister and deputy First Minister becoming a Statutory Committee, bringing the total number to eleven. This committee was established to give advice and assistance to the First Minister and deputy First Minister, to help them carry out their responsibilities. On 12th April 2010, the Justice Committee was added, as Justice became an additional Stormont government department. Policing and Criminal Law had previously been a reserved matter but was transferred to the Assembly on this date.

Statutory Committees have the following powers:

1. They can examine government departments and give advice, perhaps on the budget or annual plan.
2. They can start the process of making new laws.
3. They can carry out investigations and produce reports, perhaps on a particular issue brought to their attention by ministers.

Statutory Committees can ask people and organisations to provide information for them in order to carry out these duties. They are made up of members of the Assembly.

- **Standing Committees** – The Assembly has established six Standing Committees to assist it in its work. They are involved with day to day issues such as finance, the use of resources and the conduct of members of the Assembly.

- **Ad Hoc Committees** – These committees are set up to do a specific piece of work, for example, a review of life sentences in prisons. They last only as long as they are needed. In the past, committees have been set up to look at the issue of flags in the community, the postal service and the criminal justice system.

The Northern Ireland Assembly has had its power suspended a number of times since devolution. When this happens, the Westminster Secretary of State for Northern Ireland takes responsibility for running each of the Northern Ireland Departments.

HOW DOES THE ASSEMBLY MAKE LAWS?

A proposal for a new law is called a **Bill**. Ministers, Committees and individual members can propose a bill to be considered by the Assembly. The Speaker introduces a Bill to the Assembly, then after debate and careful thought, a vote is taken. If the Bill is approved, then the Speaker of the Assembly will ask the Secretary of State to seek Royal Assent to enable the Bill to become an **Act of the Northern Ireland Assembly**.

ACTIVITY

PROPOSE A BILL AND MAKE A LAW

- Work in a group with about 3 or 4 other students. You have to decide on a bill to propose to the class. You could consider the following questions:

    1. Why do we need this new rule?
    2. Who will this new rule affect?
    3. How will we enforce this new rule?

- There will then need to be class debate. Which of the proposed bills should be introduced as a new law?

- The next stage is a class vote. If a bill is accepted, the teacher can be asked to make it law!

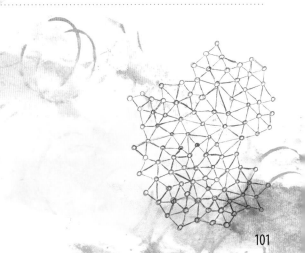

WHAT IS THE ROLE OF THE EXECUTIVE COMMITTEE?

The Executive Committee has special responsibilities and it is similar to the Cabinet in Westminster. It is made up of the **First Minister** and **deputy First Minister** and there is also a Minister for each of the 11 government departments. The Ministers are appointed from the 108 MLAs on the Assembly and these responsibilities are given out fairly according to how many seats each party won in the Assembly elections. The Executive Committee brings forward suggestions for new legislation in the form of Bills. It also sets out a Programme for Government each year, with a proposed budget.

The 11 government departments, with some of their main responsibilities, are as follows:

Agriculture and Rural Development:
Fishing, farming and countryside issues.

Culture, Arts and Leisure:
Museums, sport and leisure facilities, festivals and music events.

Education: Schools and youth services.

Employment and Learning: Further Education and unemployment.

Enterprise, Trade and Investment: Promoting local business and creating employment.

Environment: Climate change, recycling, pollution and water quality.

Finance and Personnel: Government spending and investments, wages for government employees.

Health, Social Services and Public Safety:
Public health issues, hospitals, health centres, care homes and provision for the mentally ill.

Justice: Policing and criminal justice.

Regional Development: Ensuring all areas have equal facilities, for example, transport and water supply.

Social Development: Housing issues, regenerating town centres and laws concerning alcoholic drink and gambling.

Each of these departments is headed by a Minister who is a member of the Executive Committee. This Minister receives help and advice from one of the Statutory Committees.

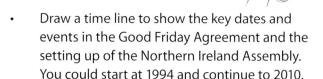

CHECK YOUR LEARNING

1. Using bullet points, give five important changes that have taken place as a result of the Good Friday Agreement.

2. Write a sentence to explain each of the following terms:
   a) Peace Process
   b) Decommissioning
   c) Referendum
   d) Devolution

3. a) When and where does the Northern Ireland Assembly meet?
   b) What powers does it have?
   c) What role does the Executive Committee have in the Assembly?

ACTIVITY

- Draw a time line to show the key dates and events in the Good Friday Agreement and the setting up of the Northern Ireland Assembly. You could start at 1994 and continue to 2010.

- Create a 'Who's Who?' of the Northern Ireland Executive Committee. You will find useful information at the following website: http://www.northernireland.gov.uk/index/your-executive.htm

In a democracy, it is important for the elected government to protect the rights of its citizens and promote inclusion and justice in society. The Northern Ireland Human Rights Commission and the Police Ombudsman's Office are working to make sure that this happens.

THE NORTHERN IRELAND HUMAN RIGHTS COMMISSION

BACKGROUND

The Northern Ireland Human Rights Commission was established by parliament through the Northern Ireland Act 1998, and it began work on 1st March 1999. Human rights and equality were seen as being central issues in the conflict in Northern Ireland, so creating a Human Rights Commission was an important outcome of the Good Friday Agreement. The NIHRC is a statutory organisation, which means it is neither a government body nor a NGO. It works independently to make sure that everyone in Northern Ireland has their human rights fully protected, through laws that are made and in the way people are treated in society. The Commission is run by a full-time Chief Commissioner and up to nine part-time commissioners. It bases all of its work on international human rights standards, including the United Nations conventions.

HOW DOES THE NIHRC PROTECT HUMAN RIGHTS?

The Northern Ireland Human Rights Commission is involved in a number of activities to promote and protect human rights. Here are some examples:

- **Promoting awareness** – It is important that people are fully informed of their rights and aware of the rights of others. The NIHRC has various ways of getting their message across such as leaflets, posters, a magazine and a website.
- **Reviewing laws** – Existing laws are reviewed on a regular basis to make sure that they are in line with international standards for human rights.
- **Advising government** – The NIHRC will advise the government on its duty to uphold human rights, and what action needs to be taken to ensure this happens.

- **Putting forward new proposals** – This might be a proposal for a new law, such as a Bill of Rights for Northern Ireland.
- **Conducting investigations** – The NIHRC investigates areas of concern, such as prison conditions or mental health care. It has the power to enter buildings of organisations that are being investigated, interview people and ask for documents.
- **Assisting individuals** – The NIHRC can help a person who believes they have suffered a human rights abuse to take their case to court.
- **Providing information and training** – The NIHRC have recently launched resources for human rights education in schools and they provide education and training on human rights.
- **Working with other organisations** – Human rights can be promoted more effectively if there is partnership with others, such as the government and NGOs.

A BILL OF RIGHTS FOR NORTHERN IRELAND

A Bill of Rights is a list of basic rights to which everyone in society is entitled to. A Bill of Rights shows that a society is committed to fairness, equality and justice for all. Many countries have a Bill of Rights in their constitution, for example, India, the USA and the Republic of Ireland.

The Good Friday Agreement promised a Bill of Rights for the people of Northern Ireland that would reflect the particular circumstances of the people who live here. The Northern Ireland Human Rights Commission was given the responsibility of advising the Secretary of State what should be in a Bill of Rights for Northern Ireland.

On 10th December 2008, the commission made a number of recommendations to the government, which included the following:

- The right to equality and prohibition of discrimination.
- The right to health.
- The right to identity and culture.
- The right to an adequate standard of living.
- Environmental rights.
- Children's rights.

© Amnesty International

A government consultation period then followed. During this time, the Human Rights Consortium, a coalition of 150 voluntary and community groups, raised awareness through a media campaign and sent information to every household. People were asked to show that they supported the proposed Bill of Rights, and there was a huge response, with over 34,000 people backing the call for a strong Bill. The consultation period ended on 31st March 2010. As of February 2011, the UK government had still not legislated for a Bill of Rights, quoting a "divergence of views" among local political parties on the issue.

SOME OTHER ISSUES OF CONCERN TO THE NIHRC

The Commission is currently involved with addressing the following infringements of human rights:

- Poverty and social exclusion.
- Racism and the protection of rights of ethnic minorities, including travellers.
- The persistence of sectarianism, leading to hate crimes and public order problems.
- The rights of women, children and immigrants in detention centres.
- Surveillance by the police and intelligence service.

The NIHRC regularly carries out research and produces reports highlighting human rights issues. Some of their past investigations have included sexual orientation, homelessness, mental health, identity cards and human trafficking.

The case study opposite is a recent example of an investigation.

CASE STUDY: INVESTIGATION INTO THE RIGHTS OF OLDER PEOPLE LIVING IN NURSING HOMES IN NORTHERN IRELAND

The number of older people in the UK is growing faster than any other age group. This has implications for the whole of society, including, among other issues, the provision of nursing care.

The Human Rights Commission is investigating how older people living in nursing homes in Northern Ireland are being treated. The NIHRC are focusing on the day to day lives of nursing home residents and the care they receive. The NIHRC ran a call for evidence through a free and confidential telephone line from 15 to 26 February 2010 and received over 200 calls from the public and those with experience of nursing care. During March 2010, they provided a short questionnaire on their website after the Freephone had closed to allow people to share their experiences of nursing homes.

The information they received through the call for evidence and their wider investigation will contribute towards a report ... It will make recommendations for improving the lives of nursing home residents as well as addressing the needs of care providers.

For more information visit: www.nihrc.org

DISCUSSION

- How important do you consider the work of the NIHRC to be?
- What are the main reasons for their effectiveness?

CHECK YOUR LEARNING

1. When was the NIHRC set up?
2. Explain why there is a need for this organisation.
3. Write a paragraph explaining how the NIHRC seeks to promote human rights in society.
4. What is the Bill of Rights? Why do some people regard a Bill of Rights as being important?

THE POLICE OMBUDSMAN'S OFFICE

BACKGROUND

The Office of the Police Ombudsman opened in November 2000. This is an organisation set up to investigate complaints from the general public about police officers in Northern Ireland. Before this, all complaints about the police were dealt with by the police, which some people did not think was fair. The Police Ombudsman's Office is an independent and unbiased system for investigating complaints against the police.

The Police Ombudsman's Office seeks to secure the confidence of both the general public and the police. It is also beneficial to both the public and the police. A person with a grievance can be assured that whatever the outcome, the issue has been dealt with fairly. If the police are found to be at fault, then action can be taken to prevent something similar happening in the future. On the other hand, if the complaint is not found to be justified, then people can be reassured that the decision is fair and not the result of a 'cover up'!

The Police Ombudsman's Office for Northern Ireland is the first completely independent service in the world for investigating complaints against the police, so it has a high standard to maintain. The Police Ombudsman's Office is paid for by the government and administered through the Northern Ireland Department of Justice. It is a good example of the government taking its responsibilities seriously in protecting citizen's rights.

MAKING A COMPLAINT

On average just over 3,000 complaints are made each year about police officers in Northern Ireland. These complaints include allegations that police officers have been rude or offensive, used unnecessary force or failed to do their job properly. However, it is important

to realise that when a complaint is made it does not necessarily mean that police have done something wrong.

The Police Ombudsman's Office will also investigate the following situations, even if a complaint has not been made:

- Any firing of a police weapon (including Taser).
- Any fatal road traffic accident involving police officers.
- Any death which might be the result of the actions of a police officer.

For most complaints there is a time limit and the Police Ombudsman's Office will only investigate complaints that have taken place within the last year. However, this does not apply to very serious or exceptional circumstances. For example, the Office has investigated many complaints from people whose relatives died during 'the troubles'.

Most of the complaints made to the Police Ombudsman's Office will be concerning the PSNI. However, it also deals with issues concerning the Larne Harbour Police, Belfast Harbour Police, the Belfast International Airport Police and the Ministry of Defence Police. It does not investigate any complaints about the army.

It does not cost anything for a member of the public to make a complaint to the Police Ombudsman's Office; the service is free, whatever the outcome.

FOLLOWING AN INVESTIGATION

Each case is investigated thoroughly. There is no set length of time for an investigation as some cases are more complicated than others. However, the Police Ombudsman's Office does aim to work as quickly as possible so people are not kept waiting longer than necessary. If the Office finds that the police have acted properly, they will give an explanation to the person who has brought the complaint. If the police are found to be at fault, the Police Ombudsman will recommend further action. This could be prosecution, a fine, dismissal or verbal warning, depending on the seriousness of the offence. Advice may also be given as to how the police can improve their services for the future. The Police Ombudsman's decision is always final, as any investigation will have been independent and unbiased.

HOW EFFECTIVE IS THE POLICE OMBUDSMAN'S OFFICE?

Al Hutchinson, Police Ombudsman for Northern Ireland:

"We provide a complaints system that is independent, impartial and effective. By doing this we can help to make sure everyone in Northern Ireland receives their entitlement to the best possible policing service."

The Police Ombudsman's Office recently carried out surveys from April 2009–March 2010 to find out how satisfied people were with their investigations. Members of the public who had made a complaint during this time were asked to fill in a questionnaire – and so were the police officers who had been investigated.

Below is a summary of their findings. Full details of all publications produced by the Office are available at: www.policeombudsman.org/publications http://www.policeombudsman.org/modules/publications/publications.cfm

Of the people who made complaints …

- 75% thought they were treated fairly by the Police Ombudsman's Office.
- Over 90% of people thought the Office staff were friendly, polite and easy to understand.
- 65% were satisfied with the outcome of their complaint, which includes 36% who were very satisfied.
- 71% said they would use the service again if the need arose.

Of the 89% of police officers who spoke to an investigator …

- 82% thought they were treated fairly by the Police Ombudsman's Office.
- 68% were satisfied with the overall service they received.
- 77% were confident that the Police Ombudsman deals with complaints in an impartial way.
- 68% thought that the police complaints system gives the police greater accountability.

The Police Ombudsman's Office is taking its role of protecting citizens' rights in Northern Ireland seriously. It attempts to provide a fair and unbiased complaints procedure which it monitors through surveys to find ways of improving the service. The following case study gives some details of a recent investigation carried out by the Police Ombudsman's Office, and the conclusion that was reached.

CASE STUDY: POLICE FAIL TO FIND BODY LYING UNDER BLANKET

The Police Ombudsman has recommended that two police officers be disciplined after a police search of a man's home in the Strathfoyle area of Derry/Londonderry failed to find his decomposed body, which was lying under a blanket on a sofa in the living room.

The man, who was dependant on alcohol, had not been seen for more than a week when police were alerted by a neighbour to concerns for his safety.

Mr Hutchinson said the circumstances of the man's death are poignant:

"I think there is a lesson for all of us in official organisations that vulnerable people, such as those dependant on alcohol, are still falling though the cracks in the system. If it was not for the persistence of the man's neighbour the discovery of his body would have been delayed even further."

The incident began on Sunday 14 September 2008 when a neighbour of the man reported she had not seen him for more than a week and said this was unusual. The woman reported the matter to police again the following day, Monday 15 September 2008 and police officers were sent to the man's home. A police officer, who was about to go inside the house, was cautioned by a colleague about the awful state of the property. Undeterred, and without either protective clothing or a torch, the officer went inside and began a search. The officer said the main living room windows were partially boarded up, the curtains were drawn and the lights were not working, all of which made visibility poor. The officers left the house without finding the body, which was under a blanket on a sofa in the room …

The Police Ombudsman, Al Hutchinson, has recommended that two police officers be disciplined: one for a failure to deal properly with the initial report made to police, the other was the police officer who carried out the initial search. Mr Hutchinson also recommended that police in the district be reminded about keeping an index of properties or locations which present issues of concern, such as health and safety issues, vicious dogs, etc.

"This would help officers by ensuring they were well informed, prepared and equipped for some of the difficult situations, they are faced with" he said.

The full report can be read on the website of the Police Ombudsman's Office:

www.policeombudsman.org

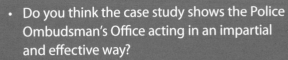

DISCUSSION

- Do you think the case study shows the Police Ombudsman's Office acting in an impartial and effective way?
- Overall, how effective do you consider the work of the Police Ombudsman's Office to be?
- Can you think of any ways in which the service could be improved?

CHECK YOUR LEARNING

1. Why was the Police Ombudsman's Office set up?
2. Give examples of some of the complaints the office deals with.
3. Write a paragraph to explain how the Police Ombudsman's Office can protect people's rights.
4. Write a paragraph to explain how the people of Northern Ireland benefit from this organisation.

EXAM FOCUS

Each chapter has focussed on exam skills. Examiners refer to these skills as Assessment Objectives. So far, we have covered:

AO1 – Demonstrating your knowledge and understanding.
AO2 – Applying your knowledge and understanding.

The final skill to practice is:

AO3 – Showing the ability to investigate, analyse and evaluate information.

Questions testing AO3 usually require a longer answer. To gain high marks you will need to write clearly, organise your material and develop your ideas. Your answer will be based partly on your own knowledge and partly on a short article you will be given to read.

The following question tests this skill:

With reference to the source below and your own knowledge assess some of the ways in which the Police Ombudsman's Office can benefit the people of Northern Ireland. [10 marks]

Source:

"Under legislation, the Police Ombudsman is obliged to put in place a police complaints system which will win the support of the public and is capable of winning the support of police officers. He is also committed to ensuring, as far as he can, that your view on this Office is based on accurate information and not on rumour, speculation or misinformation. In January 2005, the Freedom of Information Act compelled organisations to make their information available to the public, unless there were reasons which exempted them from doing so."

http://www.policeombudsman.org/modules/pages/information.cfm

ed to each

vailable

GLOSSARY

ACCESSION: This term can be used when a newcomer becomes a member of an established group; for example, when a country joins the European Economic Union it is said to have accession to the EEC.

BOYCOTT: This refers to a complete refusal to buy a product or take part in an activity as a way of registering a protest.

CENSUS: The official counting of the population, carried out by the government every 10 years.

CONFLICT RESOLUTION: This refers to a range of methods for eliminating sources of conflict. It usually involves people talking to each other and working out a solution that is acceptable to everybody involved.

CONSTITUENCY: A constituency is an area represented by a member of parliament (MP). The majority of people living in this area will have voted for this person the last time an election was held.

CULTURAL DIVERSITY: This term can be applied to a society where the people come from many different ethnic groups.

DECOMMISSION: To remove something from active service and no longer use it. In the Northern Ireland Peace Process, this term usually refers to weapons.

DEMOCRACY: A system of rule that should give equality and freedom to all citizens, and where everyone has equal access to power.

DEVOLUTION: This is a transfer of power from a higher level (such as the national government) to a lower level (such as the government of a particular region). Devolution can give greater responsibility to regional governments without the national government giving up its overall authority.

DISCRIMINATION: This means to be treated in a less favourable way than other people. It includes the workplace, at school or having access to important services, such as healthcare.

ECONOMIC POLICY: This term refers to the action that a government might take in order to manage the country's money efficiently. This can involve setting interest rates and deciding on the government budget. The aim is for businesses to make a profit and for people's living standards to get better.

EQUAL OPPORTUNITY: Everyone has the same chance as everyone else to receive an education or promotion at work. For example, a person should never be treated unfairly because of factors such as gender, age, race, religion or disability.

ETHNIC GROUP: This is any group of people with a distinct cultural identity. Ethnicity can be defined by race, religion, language, food, music and traditions.

ETHNIC MINORITY: This is any ethnic group who are relatively small in number in the area where they are living.

HATE CRIME: This is a criminal offence mainly motivated by the victim being different to the attacker. This difference could be because of race, ethnicity, sexual orientation or religious belief, for example.

LEGAL OBLIGATION: An action which must be carried out or a service that must be provided, as there is a law in place to make sure this happens.

LEGISLATION: This term refers to laws which have been made by the government.

LOBBYING: This involves bringing an issue to the attention of a local councillor, MLA or MP to encourage them to take action.

MANIFESTO: A document in which a political party sets out their beliefs and policies.

MARGINALISED: This term refers to a person, or group of people, made to feel that they are excluded from society and therefore cannot play a full role.

MEDIATION: This involves helping people to communicate on a difficult issue. A 'mediator' who will not be seen as taking sides is usually involved to improve understanding between the two groups and help them talk to each other.

NON-GOVERNMENTAL ORGANISATION (NGO): A group that does not receive government funding and operates independently. Alternative names are 'Voluntary Organisation' or 'Charity'.

PREJUDICE: The word 'prejudice' literally means to 'pre-judge' someone. Prejudice is therefore a judgement based on ignorance.

PRESSURE GROUP: An organised group of people who aim to influence government policy, or the laws that they pass.

PUBLIC AUTHORITY: This is a group or organisation, such as a local council or Education and Library Board, which has been given official power to govern or administrate in the local community.

PUBLIC SERVICES: This term refers to the services provided by the government to its citizens, such as education, healthcare, repairs to roads and collection of household waste.

RACISM: Racism is the belief that one race of people is superior to another. Racism can involve discrimination because of factors such as skin colour, language, nationality and culture.

REFERENDUM: An election where all eligible citizens have the chance to vote.

SANCTION: This is an official action taken against a country to force it to obey international law. A sanction usually involves stopping trade, so the country cannot import any goods or sell its exports.

SCAPEGOAT: A scapegoat is someone who is blamed for the wrongs someone else has committed.

SECTARIANISM: This is prejudice or discrimination directed towards someone who is a member of a smaller group within the same race or nationality.

SOCIAL EQUALITY: Having equal rights under the law, such as the right to vote, own property and have freedom of speech. It also includes access to health care, education and other social services.

SOCIAL JUSTICE: Describes the movement towards a world which is fairer for all its citizens. It includes the idea that everyone is entitled to the same basic human rights, which should be available for everyone.

STEREOTYPE: This is a crude mental picture that a person might have of someone from another culture. Stereotypes often assume that everyone from a particular group has the same characteristics.

'THE TROUBLES': The troubles in Northern Ireland refers to the three decades of violence that took place towards the end of the last century. This was largely between the Roman Catholic nationalist community and the Protestant unionist community.

INDEX

COPYRIGHT INFORMATION

Copyright has been acknowledged to the best of our ability. If there are any inadvertent errors or omissions, we shall be happy to correct them in any future editions.

Acknowledgements

The following questions are included with the permission of the Northern Ireland Council for the Curriculum, Examinations and Assessment:

GCSE Learning for Life and Work Modular Specimen Assessment Materials, Unit 3: Local and Global Citizenship Specimen Paper (2009); GCSE Learning for Life and Work Modular Paper, Unit 3: Local and Global Citizenship Summer 2010, GLW41. © 2009-2010

Thanks to the following organisations and copyright holders for their kind permission to use their logos, titles, images and information:

Amnesty International, ArtsEkta, Belfast Cathedral, Big Lottery Fund, FAIRTRADE, Friends of the Earth NI, Irish Sikh Council, NICEM, NICVA, NIHRC, OXFAM GB and OXFAM Ireland, Police Ombudsman's Office, Save the Children, TIDY Northern Ireland, WAR ON WANT NI, The Equality Commission for Northern Ireland.

'QUIZ: DEALING WITH DISASTERS – WHAT WOULD YOU DO?' on page 88 is adapted by the publisher from 'Dealing with Disasters, Lesson Plan 3: Disaster Strikes', 2007-2008, with the permission of Oxfam GB, Oxfam House, John Smith Drive, Cowley, Oxford OX4 2JY, UK

www.oxfam.org.uk/education. Oxfam GB does not necessarily endorse any text or activities that accompany the materials, nor has it approved the adapted text.

The following images are licensed under the GNU Free Documentation License. Permission is granted to copy, distribute and/or modify this document under the terms of the GNU Free Documentation License, Version 1.2 or any later version published by the Free Software Foundation; with no Invariant Sections, no Front-Cover Texts. A copy of the license can be viewed at http://www.gnu.org/licenses/fdl.html

Pages 7 (bottom right), 49

The following images are licensed under the Creative Commons Attribution 3.0 Unported License. Permission is granted to share and/or remix this work providing the work is attributed in the manner specified by the author or licensor. A copy of this license can be viewed at http://creativecommons.org/licenses/by-sa/3.0/deed.en

Cover (left), Pages 5 (far right), 5 (middle right), 5 (middle left), 7 (bottom right), 14 (bottom left), 14 (top left), 15 (right), 22, 23 (bottom collage, right image), 23 (bottom collage, left image), 31 (middle), 31 (top left), 31 (top right), 31 (bottom left), 49, 100

Picture credits

All photographs are by iStock Photo except for the following which are included with kind permission of the copyright holders. The numbers denote page numbers.

Amnesty International: 78, 104
Amru Zainal Abidin: 15 (right)
Amy (Little Red Pen): 5 (far right)
Austin Osuide: 31 (top left)
Belfast Cathedral: 35 (left)
Ben Chaney: 5 (middle right)
Big Lottery Fund: 26
Bill Fromesm: 23 (bottom collage, left image)

Brendan Lally: 8 (bottom right)
Connor Smith: 9 (right, both)
Denlander: 7 (bottom right)
Eileen Chan-Hu, Chief Executive, Chinese Welfare Association: 6 (right)
George Keith: 14 (bottom left)
John Benson: 14 (top left)
Liam Hughes: 12 (bottom left)
Dr Mamoun Mobayed: 19 (bottom left)
Henry Doggart©ArtSEkta: 13 (top right), 14 (top right)
Malcolm Johnston: 38 (bottom left), 39
Nigel Wilson: 31 (middle)
Neil Rickards: 12 (top left and top right)
Neo-Jay: 49
Parkway Photography: 75
Patrick Feller: 22

Port of San Diego: 38 (top left)
Rachel Irwin: 27 (top)
Rick Harris: 5 (middle left)
Robert Paul Young: cover (left), 23 (bottom collage), 100
Ronnie Moore©ArtsEkta: 13 (middle right)
Sam Wennerlund: 12 (middle left)
Save the Children: 86 (all)
Sdo216: 31 (top right)
Shutterstock: 7 (top left)
Steindy: 31 (bottom left)
Tony Moorey: 97 (right)
US Library of Congress Prints and Photographs Division: 96 (second from bottom)
War on Want NI: 92 (bottom), 93 (left)